JELLY ROLL™

QUILT MAGIC

KIMBERLY EINMO

AQS Publishing

Located in Paducah, Kentucky, the American Quilter's Society (AQS) is dedicated to promoting the accomplishments of today's quilters. Through its publications and events, AQS strives to honor today's quilt-makers and their work and to inspire future creativity and innovation in quiltmaking.

Executive Book Editor: Andi Milam Reynolds
Senior Editor: Linda Baxter Lasco
Graphic Design: Lynda Smith
Cover Design: Michael Buckingham
Quilt Photography: Charles R. Lynch
How-to Photography: Kimberly Einmo (pages 3, 15, 21, 25, 29–30, 68, 75, 79, 84-85)
Additional Photography: Thilo Schüller (page 74) and Alisha Pergola (pages 2, 4, 6, 10, 16, 20, 39, 60–61, 69, 71, 80, 86, 95)

Additional copies of this book may be ordered from the American Quilter's Society, PO Box 3290, Paducah, KY 42002-3290, or online at www.AmericanQuilter.com.

Text ©2011, Author, Kimberly Einmo
Artwork ©2011, American Quilter's Society

Library of Congress Cataloging-in-Publication Data

Einmo, Kimberly.
  Jelly roll quilt magic / by Kimberly Einmo.
    p. cm.
  ISBN 978-1-60460-000-1
  1. Quilting--Patterns. 2. Patchwork--Patterns. 3. Patchwork quilts. I. Title.
TT835.E4469 2011
746.46'041--dc23
                    2011033785

American Quilter's Society
P. O. Box 3290 • Paducah, KY 42002-3290
www.AmericanQuilter.com

DEDICATION

I dedicate this book to my best friend and devoted husband of 22 years, Kent; to our handsome sons who are growing up to be fine young men of integrity, Joshua and Andrew; and to my loving parents, Bill and Nina Wallace. Your support and encouragement has allowed me to follow my dreams around the world. I am supremely grateful for the laughter and joy you bring into my life. From the bottom of my heart, I thank you all.

KIMBERLY'S CREED

I love life—everything it has to offer and the endless possibilities of each new day. I especially love to quilt and to share my passion and enthusiasm for quilting with everyone!

FUN FACT: Kent is the CEO of my fun little business. CEO stands for Carries Everything Out!

Acknowledgments

Writing a book is a major undertaking. Writing a book with quilting projects and patterns is an undertaking of mammoth proportions. It takes time to design the quilts themselves, gather the materials, figure the math, write the patterns, make the quilts, and finally, combine everything together into a working manuscript. While I love each and every aspect of the book-writing process, it can be daunting. That's why I'm blessed to have a small group of true blue, talented and dedicated friends who always "have my back." These gals have not only been my friends for years, they have worked tirelessly behind the scenes to come through for me to road test the patterns, make some of the quilts, do some of the machine quilting, and even bind some of the quilts. This book simply wouldn't have come together without their willing support and talented stitching skills. The words "thank you" hardly seem adequate to express my gratitude! If you see them, be sure to thank them for me!

Birgit Schüller   Carolyn Archer   Carla Conner
Claire Neal   Christine LaCroix   Judy Schrader
Ilona Baumhofer   Miriam Fay

I'd like to sincerely thank my publisher, Meredith Schroeder, my editors, Andi Reynolds and Linda Lasco, graphic designer Lynda Smith, and all the talented people at the American Quilter's Society for their amazing ability to capture my words and personality and help translate them onto the pages of this book so beautifully. Since my association began with these wonderful folks back in 2004, my respect and admiration for them has only grown through the years. I consider them as part of my extended family and I truly look forward to seeing them every time our paths cross at shows and events around the country. I'm absolutely blessed to be associated with such a terrific group of exceptional people!

And last but most assuredly not least, I'd like to thank the ultra-talented gal behind the lens of the camera who took many of the photos you see in this book, Alisha Pergola. We had such an amazing, fun-filled day during the photo shoot and she truly captured the joy and just plain silliness of our family through her camera lens. Thank you, Alisha!

TABLE OF CONTENTS

INTRODUCTION

It all began with a phone call late in 2008 from my editor, Andi Reynolds, who had a special request. "Would you consider designing quilts and writing a book using Jelly Rolls?" I heard myself answer her with an enthusiastic, "Sure!" Then, as I hung up the phone, I thought, "Oh no. What on earth have I just committed to do?"

Panic didn't set in right away even though the logistics alone were difficult. We were living in Germany at the time and it wasn't as if I could run down to the local quilt shop (because there wasn't one) and pick up several bundles of Jelly Rolls and start cutting. Jelly Rolls were still fairly new on the quilting scene in the United States but they were absolutely unheard of in Europe! I emailed my friend and contact at Moda Fabrics, Lissa Alexander, and asked if she would send me a variety of Jelly Rolls.

The holidays came and went that year and finally a big box of fabric bundles from Moda arrived on my doorstep in early January. I was nervous and excited as I unpacked the box and set those delicious bundles of tempting textile treats in a pleasing display on my cutting table. By golly, they sure looked pretty sitting there. I stood back and looked at the enticing stacks of eye candy artfully arranged. Aaahhhh. Then, I began to panic.

Feeling something akin to writer's block, those bundles sat there day after day while I tried to decide just how I was going to use them. I successfully procrastinated for the next three weeks, every once in awhile tiptoeing past my studio door and peeking in at the cutting table. Yep, the Jelly Rolls were still sitting there, a pretty still life portrait. Finally I realized I was going to have to deal with those bundles head on.

Now here's the big secret in quilt-land nobody ever tells you about Jelly Rolls. When you untie the bow and remove the rubber band holding all those strips neatly rolled together, KA-BOOM! There is an explosion of fabric—two and a half yards to be exact—that bursts forth from those bundles, never to be neatly rolled again! I had opened Pandora's box and there was no turning back.

I gave myself a pep talk and dove in head first. And the rest, as they say, is history. Once I got going, I had momentum on my side. Within a week I had enough designs to fill a book. It was even more fun to cut and sew the strips and create the quilts themselves than it was to design them. To finally see the book come together was the best part of all!

Jelly Roll Quilts and More was released on January 1, 2010, by the American Quilter's Society and instantly became their #1 best-seller. (I'm still blushing and dancing the happy dance!) But here's the really neat thing: I haven't stopped designing quilts using those fabric rolls of calorie-free goodness. The effortlessly blended bundles of strips are just so easy to use. I simply keep finding more fun ways to use them in quiltmaking.

If you're a Jelly Roll rookie, let me assure you that in no time at all you'll be a seasoned veteran. Whether you use pre-packaged Jelly Rolls or strips cut from fabrics from your own stash, you'll discover why they are so addictive and simply wonderful for quiltmaking!

As long as precut fabric bundles continue to thrive, I'll continue to find exciting new ways to use them in my quilts! So I hope you'll join me in creating some of your own Jelly Roll magic! The possibilities are endless!

GET READY...

You probably want to jump right in and sew, but take a little time to read this chapter first!

This book isn't written like most other pattern or project books. As with my previous book, I've written this in the first person so it will feel as if I'm talking with YOU! Consider me your own personal quilting coach! I've infused the chapters with a sense of fun combined with lots of tips to teach you new techniques and ways to effectively use those fabulous precut fabric bundles to make spectacular quilts.

There's a lot of new information to cover so I've divided this book into manageable sections so quilters of all skill levels will find it easy to use and to improve their skills along the way. I don't want to waste valuable time (yours) or space (book pages are expensive real estate), so I'll briefly review the basics of what you'll need to do to get started.

For a more thorough review of quiltmaking basics, let me encourage you to refer to the Get Ready chapter of my previous book, *Jelly Roll Quilts and More*. For those of you who already own the book, reading it again will be a quick refresher and a great way to step up to the next level of quilting with Jelly Rolls, Layer Cakes, and other precuts. If you don't already own a copy, let me encourage you to get one for yourself—either borrow one from a friend or order your own signed and personalized copy from my website, **www.kimberlyeinmo.com**. You'll be glad you did.

What You'll Need: fabrics, tools, and basic supplies, short and sweet!

A place to sew—Whether you have your own spacious sewing studio or you're using the family dining room table in between meals, keep your sewing area organized and well-stocked with quality supplies and keep them handy as you cut and stitch.

A good chair—A chair with proper back support is essential for hours of pain-free sewing at your machine. Invest in one if you don't have one already. It's worth it.

Good lighting—Proper lighting is as important as proper back support. Natural lighting is ideal, but if you sew in the evening or you don't have access to good natural light, find the best lights you can and make your sewing area as bright as the surface of the sun! (Well, almost....)

A sewing machine in good working condition—If your sewing machine doesn't work properly, no amount of preparation or quality supplies will help. You'll end up frustrated and discouraged. Have your machine serviced regularly and clean the lint build-up EVERY time you change the bobbin.

Specialty sewing feet—At the very least, you'll need the following accessory feet to construct the quilts in this book:

Piecing foot (¼" foot)	Open-toe appliqué foot
Walking foot	Free-motion foot

Rotary cutter—You'll want to use a variety of sizes to accurately cut the pieces for these magical quilts. I recommend having three sizes: 18mm, 45mm, and 60mm. However, if you only have access to just one rotary cutter, use a 45mm rotary cutter.

Rotary blades—It is essential to use a new, sharp blade! Change the blade for each new large project, or as soon as it starts to be difficult to cut. Change the blade sooner should it develop a burr and begin to skip threads or cut inaccurately.

Self-healing rotary-cutting mat—Use a mat that isn't warped or deeply grooved from hours (or years!) of use. And use a mat with measurement lines. Remember—they put those lines on the mat for a reason. Measure twice, cut once!

Machine needles—In general, use a size 75/11 Quilting needle for piecing. You can use the same size needle for machine quilting or one matched appropriately to the type of thread you are using. It is wise to keep a stash of extra needles on hand and change them frequently!

Iron—Use an iron with plenty of steam and keep the sole plate shiny and clean. Remember, steam is your friend!

Ironing surface—A sturdy ironing board is essential. One that adjusts to fit your height is a blessing.

Fabric—Use high-quality 100 percent cotton.

Thread—Use a 50-wt. thread for piecing the quilts. The options are almost endless for the type of threads you can use for quilting. Do your homework and make test samples before using any threads on your actual quilts.

Batting—There are many batting types to choose from. I tend to use wool (which resists creasing) and the new bamboo batting. Test the various types and choose the batting that works best for you!

Scissors—You'll need shears and sharp snips for clipping threads.

Seam ripper—You'll need one of these at some point, so make sure you use one that is not rusty or broken as it could cause damage to your fabrics.

Specialty rulers—Over the years, I have designed a number of rulers and acrylic tools that feature no math, no wasted fabric, and no-stress techniques. They truly help quilters get the most bang for their buck especially when using precuts. I've included these rulers (and one invented by another designer) plus some additional tools in the instructions with diagrams of how to use them.

EZ Flying Geese ruler   EZ Jelly Roll Ruler
Tri-Recs Tools   Easy Hearts Tool

Acrylic rulers—At the very least, you'll need an acrylic ruler 6½" x 24½". However, a 12½" square ruler is extremely helpful for squaring up your blocks. If you have other sizes of rulers, use them to help make cutting easier and more efficient.

Straight pins—I prefer the long, flat, flower head pins for pinning the seams. They are relatively inexpensive, so if your straight pins are short, rusty, or bent, throw them out and splurge on a new box.

Marking tools—A mechanical pencil, disappearing blue ink pen, and rolling chalk markers are very helpful. I especially like the new pens whose ink disappears from friction or heat, available at quilt shops or office supply stores.

Basting tools—You'll likely need basting safety pins or a basting gun to help you baste your quilts for machine quilting (unless you're planning on enlisting the services of a longarm quilter).

Fusible web—Buy it from the bolt whenever possible. Never use fusible web that is old or brittle.

Stabilizers—You'll need a temporary or "tear-away" type of stabilizer for the machine appliqué.

Basic sewing supplies—Keep a fully stocked sewing box or bin full of basic sewing supplies handy at all times. It will save you hours of searching in vain for items you need close at hand.

A longarm machine quilter—If you don't quilt your own quilts, find someone you trust to quilt them for you. She (or he) is probably going to be your new best friend. When you finish piecing your quilts you can move on to the next project as soon as you send your top out the door to be quilted.

Brief History of Precuts

Moda Fabrics first introduced Jelly Rolls in October 2006 at Quilt Market in Houston. They set off a frenzy and turned the quilting community upside down with excitement! In the months and years since their debut, a Jelly Roll has come to be known as any group of 40 strips measuring 2½" wide. Just about every fabric manufacturer has introduced their own version.

Moda Fabrics didn't stop with Jelly Rolls. Soon, they introduced Honey Buns, Layer Cakes, Cupcakes, Dessert Rolls, Turnovers, and more. Although many people thought these pint-sized goodies were simply a fad, they have proven to have incredible staying power. People everywhere are jumping on board this textile treat wagon to create beautiful quilts and crafts from these highly versatile bundles. Precuts certainly show no signs of slowing down in popularity!

Precuts 101

Precut	Size	Total Yardage (approximate)	
Fat Quarters	18" x 24"	¼ yard each piece. Total yardage varies on the number of fat quarters	
Jelly Roll—40 strips	2½" x 42"	2½ yards	
Honey Bun—40 strips	1½" x 42"	1⅔ yards	
Layer Cake—40 squares	10" x 10"	2½ yards	
Charm Squares (also called Cupcakes)	5" x 5"	Depends on the number of squares per pack	
Turnovers	6" half-square triangles	Depends on the number of triangles per pack	
Dessert Roll—40 strips	5" x 42"	5 yards	
Candy Bars—40 rectangles	2½" x 5"	½ yard	
Petit Fours—40 squares	2½" x 2½"	¼ yard	

Jelly Rolls: So, what's all the fuss about?

For those of you have never used any of these precut fabric wonders, you might be wondering why there is so much excitement. It's simple. Once you use a Jelly Roll you'll know. There is so much to love!

@ They are an economical way to sample each piece from a fabric line.

@ 2½" strips are the single most versatile width used in quiltmaking.

@ They are completely portable and easy to tote.

@ They store easily and neatly in your stash (until you take off that ribbon holding the strips together!).

@ The design opportunities are limitless.

@ They save preparation time; you can dive right into your project and get to the good stuff!

@ Your quilts will be scrappy yet beautifully coordinated.

@ They are great fun to collect!

How do you Prewash Precuts?

The simple truth is, you don't prewash your precuts. It just isn't practical. I tried putting 40 Jelly Roll strips into the washing machine once. Trust me when I tell you it wasn't a pretty sight. They all came through the spin cycle like a wound-up, mangled mess of tightly twisted threads that were practically impossible to untangle.

I realize there are purists out there who have always pre-washed their fabrics before cutting and using them in their quilts and if you are one of those folks, I imagine you are squirming in your seat right about now. Believe me when I tell you that I empathize with how you're feeling.

I, too, was always one of those prewashing purists. When I first began working with precut bundles, I had to take long, deep breaths to steady my nerves before I could actually pick up a rotary cutter and cut into an unwashed Jelly Roll strip. But once I got into the process, I realized it was not only okay to *not* prewash my precuts, it was, in fact rather liberating! And I have never had any trouble with my precut fabrics bleeding or running.

Making Your Own Precuts

You don't need to buy any precut bundles to make these delectable calorie-free delights. Create your own!

I'll bet the majority of you reading this right now have a fantastic stash or a scrap basket overflowing with bits and schniblets of fabric too wonderful to discard just waiting to be repurposed! This is a fantastic opportunity for you to do some serious stash busting or scrap reduction.

Here are some great ideas for making do with what you already have while not spending one extra cent!

@ Simply cut usable 2½" strips (Jelly Rolls), 5" x 5" squares (Charms), or 10" x 10" squares (Layer Cakes) from the fabrics you already have on hand!

@ Cut at least one 2½" strip from every fabric you have in your stash and group them by colors or value.

@ Host a stash-busting, strip swap party with your friends or guild members.

@ Convert your scraps, fat quarter bundles, and other odd yardage amounts to 2½" strips, 5" squares, and 2½" x 5" rectangles. Then organize the rest of your stash with the larger yardage pieces.

@ Cut up the "ugly" fabrics in your stash. Suddenly, they won't seem so ugly anymore and will add just the right amount of sparkle to your quilts. Seriously, this works!

@ Break down the task of cutting strips into small, manageable steps. Focus on one color group per day or one box or shelf of fabric at a time.

@ Invite a friend to join you. Twice the productivity and twice the fun! Offer to let her take home half of everything she cuts. (Then go to her house and reverse the process!)

An Extra Treat—Recipes

I've included mention of some of my all-time favorite recipes and direct you to my website (www.kimberlyeinmo. com) to find them. "Why?" you may ask. By popular demand! Seriously, while I'm not a chef like Ina Garten (although I certainly fancy myself as "The Barefoot Quiltessa"), I have received so many emails and comments from people telling me they love the fact that I shared my time-honored, family-tested, and quilter-friendly recipes in my last book. I simply just had to share a few more this time!

Get Set...
Top Tips and Techniques to Make Your Own Jelly Roll Magic!

Abbreviations

You'll need to know the abbreviations I use throughout the book.

HST—half-square triangle
QST—quarter-square triangle
RST—right sides together
WST—wrong sides together
LOF—length of fabric
RSU—right side up
RSD—right side down
WOF—width of fabric

How to Construct the Units

Mastering a few fundamental cutting and piecing skills to get the most out of precut fabrics is easy! If you can cut and piece a few basic units, you can construct a wide variety of different size blocks and create an unlimited number of exciting and dynamic quilt layouts! It's fun, economical, and great for stash busting.

You can make all the blocks in this book using specialty rulers designed for efficiency and to save fabric or you can use more traditional techniques. Choose your method and let's get started!

How to make half-square triangles (HSTs) using the EZ Flying Geese ruler

Place 2 fabric strips RST (right sides together).

NOTE: If you are right handed, begin cutting on the left side of the strip unit and cut from left to right. If you are left handed, begin cutting on the right side of the strip unit and cut from right to left.

Use Side B (mint green side) of the ruler to cut triangle units from the fabric strips, rotating ruler as shown.

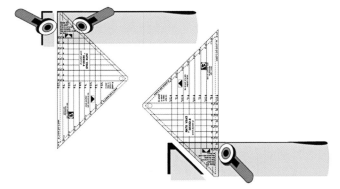

Keep fabric units RST and stitch ¼" on the long side of triangles.

Press the seams closed first, then press seam allowance toward darker fabric.

Trim the dog ears from the end of the HST (half-square triangle) unit.

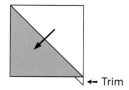

← Trim

Can you make HSTs from 2½" strips using a traditional method? Of course!

How to make HSTs using the traditional method

Cut 2 squares 2½" x 2½" from 2 different Jelly Roll strips.

Draw a diagonal line on the back of the lighter square.

Place the squares RST and stitch on the drawn line.

Trim the seam ¼" from the stitching line and discard the small triangles.

Press the unit with the seam allowance toward the darker triangle.

Stitching ↑
Line

Trim ¼"
seam allowance

↙ Press

How to make Flying Geese units using the EZ Flying Geese ruler

Cut fabric strips according to the finished size of Flying Geese units shown on the left side of Side A (magenta pink side) of the ruler.

NOTE: You can cut through two or four layers of fabric strips without slippage. Six or more layers result in a loss of cutting accuracy.

Use Side A to cut the center triangle (the QST "goose") from the strips.

Rotate the ruler along the strip to cut the desired number of "goose" pieces.

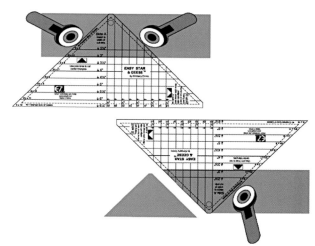

Fold another fabric strip RST and use Side B (mint green) to cut the HST "wings" from the strips. This results in mirror-image wings.

Sew a B side triangle to an A center triangle unit by matching notched edge to notched edge and pointed edge to pointed edge, using a ¼" seam. Press the unit closed first; then press it open with the seam allowance toward the wing.

Sew a B triangle to other side of the A center triangle. Press the seam allowance toward the B triangle wing.

NOTE: Seam allowances must always be pressed away from the center triangle!

Trim the "dog ears" on the sides. Square-up the units if necessary.

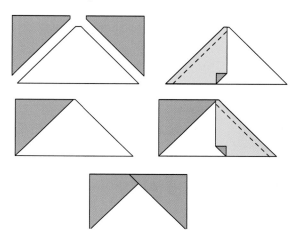

EZ Flying Geese Ruler Handy
Strip Reference Chart

Strip Width	# of Triangles from Side A (QSTs)	# of Triangles from Side B (HSTs)
2½	14	24
3	11	22
3½	9	20
4	8	18
4½	7	16
5	7	13
5½	6	12
6	5	10
6½	5	10

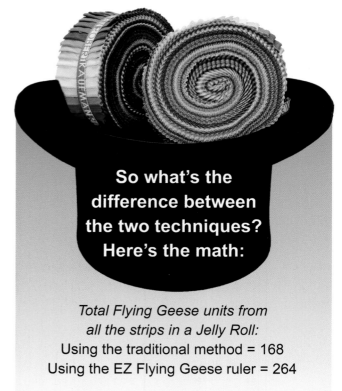

So what's the difference between the two techniques? Here's the math:

Total Flying Geese units from all the strips in a Jelly Roll:
Using the traditional method = 168
Using the EZ Flying Geese ruler = 264

Bottom line: You can make 96 more Flying Geese units from a Jelly Roll pack using the EZ Flying Geese ruler than by using the traditional method.

How to make Flying Geese units using the traditional method

Cut one 2½" x 4½" rectangle and two 2½" x 2½" squares.

Draw a diagonal line on the backs of the squares. One at a time, place a square RST on the rectangle and stitch on the drawn line.

Trim ¼" beyond the stitching line and press the seam allowance away from the rectangle.

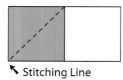 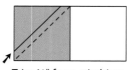

Stitching Line

Trim ¼" from stitching line and discard extra fabric

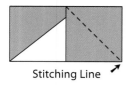 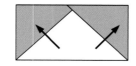

Stitching Line

How to use the EZ Jelly Roll Ruler

When creating the quilts for *Jelly Roll Quilts & More*, I realized I hardly ever made cuts in ⅛" increments and I cut the same sizes repeatedly. I also realized I worked many late night hours and my eyes don't focus quite as well as they used to, especially at night.

With these things in mind, I designed a ruler to work easily and efficiently with all precuts: the EZ Jelly Roll Ruler. The 5" x 10" size of this ruler instantly makes it one half of a Layer Cake. The mint green markings show up well on all fabrics so you can cut your strips and squares into manageable units in a snap.

Can you use other rotary rulers with eighth-inch measurements on your precuts? Of course you can! But I think that once you start using this handy-dandy ruler, it will soon become your favorite "go-to" ruler for cutting squares, rectangles, and diamonds from precuts, along with a thousand other things as well.

How to cut squares:

Line up the mint green highlight line along the horizontal edge of your precut strip matching the width of your strip.

Cut a square.

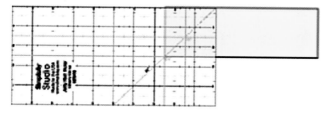

How to cut rectangles:

Line up the mint green highlight line along the bottom edge of your precut strip matching the width of your strip.

Use the ¼", ½", or whole inch markings to cut the length of your desired unit size. Cut a rectangle.

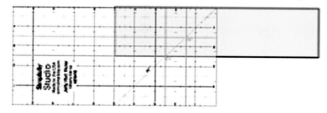

How to cut diamonds:

Line up the 45-degree line along the bottom horizontal edge of your fabric strip. Trim off the first triangle.

Slide the ruler over to the cutting line on the ruler that matches the width of fabric strip and cut a diamond.

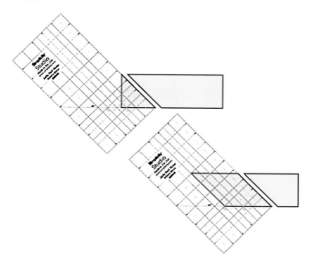

EZ Jelly Roll Ruler Handy Strip and Square Reference Table

Here are two more charts you'll definitely want to keep within easy reach. They will help you calculate the number of basic patches you can cut from strips (based on a 40" strip) and precut squares. Use this chart to easily convert commercial patterns to help you avoid wasting any fabric from your precuts!

Unit Size	# of Units from a 5" x 5" Square (Charm Pack)	# of Units from a 10" x 10" Square (Layer Cake)
1½" x 1½"	9	36
2½" x 2½"	4	16
2½" x 5"	2	8
5" x 5"	1	4
5" x 10"	0	2

Strip Width	Unit Size	# of Units from 40" Strip
1½"	1½" x 1½"	26
	1½" x 2"	20
	1½" x 2½"	16
	1½" x 3"	13
	1½" x 3½"	11
	1½" x 4"	10
	1½" x 4½"	8
	1½" x 5"	8
	1½" x 5½"	7
2½"	2½" x 2½"	16
	2½" x 3"	13
	2½" x 3½"	11
	2½" x 4"	10
	2½" x 4½"	8
	2½" x 5"	8
	2½" x 5½"	7

How to use the Tri-Recs Tools

I frequently use this ruler set to make those pesky star points for blocks such as 54-40 or Fight. Like my rulers, they are designed to work well with strips in half- and whole-inch increments, so they are perfect to use with Jelly Roll strips. Try them—I think you'll like them as much as I do. Once again, these specialty tools allow you to get the most out of precuts without wasting any fabric.

Cut fabric strips ½" wider than the finished size of Tri-Recs units. Lay the top edge of the Tri or Recs tool along the top edge of the strip and align the bottom of the strip with the appropriate line on the ruler. Cut on both sides.

Rotate the tool and align with the strip edge and cut again.

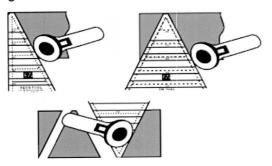

With RST, lay one Recs triangle on the left side of the Tri triangle as shown. Align the angle on the Recs triangle with the bottom of the Tri triangle. Press the seam allowance toward the Recs unit. Add the other Recs unit in same manner. Stitch and press. Trim the dog ears on the corners.

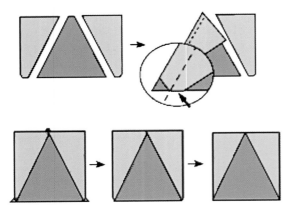

To piece double rectangle units, place two Recs units RST and align the angles as shown. Stitch and press toward the darker rectangle. Trim the dog ears on the corners.

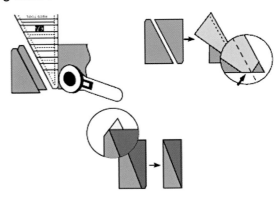

A Quick Geometry Lesson: Triangles 101

I simply love triangles! Triangles are the zing in blocks that make quilts dazzle with excitement! Next to the square, they are arguably the most necessary and useful of all basic quilting shapes.

You may have struggled with geometry class in high school, but as a quilter you need to know the basic principles of triangles and how they affect your blocks! Triangles can behave like rowdy kids; they can act up at the most inopportune times, causing seams to curve and blocks to ripple.

How are half-square and quarter-square triangles different and why does it matter?

To begin, let's consider the square—one that has been cut on the straight of grain, as most squares are. If you cut a square once diagonally, you get two triangles. The straight of grain runs along the two short sides of the triangle, with the bias edge on the long side. These triangles are half-square triangles because both halves came from one square.

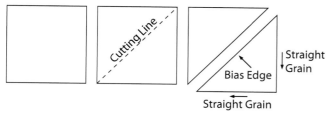

On half-square triangles, the straight of grain is on the short sides and the bias is on the long side.

Let's consider the same square now cut twice diagonally. You get four triangles. Now the straight of grain is on the long side of the triangle and the bias edges are on the two shorter sides. These triangles are quarter-square triangles because four triangles came from one square.

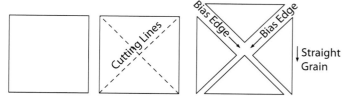

On quarter-square triangles, the straight of grain is on the long side and the bias is on the short sides.

This information about the bias and straight of the grain is important when placing triangles within blocks. The rule of thumb is this: In most cases the straight of grain in every triangle needs to run along the outside edge of the completed block, although there are exceptions to every rule.

So, now you have mastered the basics of Triangles 101. Well done! Don't be intimidated by triangles. Use them to your advantage, and make your quilts spectacular!

Try This!
Fast fuzz reduction with a lint roller.

For anyone who's ever untied a Jelly Roll, you know what happens. And if you haven't untied one yet, well, let's just say you'll soon find out. POOF! In an instant it looks as though a lint bomb blew up all over you and the room where you're standing. Those zillion tiny bits of fabric crumbs go everywhere! It might just possibly be the one and only thing I don't like about Jelly Rolls!

But never fear! I've come up with a brilliant way to reduce the lint explosion by more than 80 percent. Use a lint roller! You know the type I'm talking about—those inexpensive rollers you can buy almost everywhere with the perforated sheets of sticky tape. So here's what you do: BEFORE you untie the bow and dig into those beautiful fabric strips, run the lint roller back and forth over both sides of your Jelly Roll. You may need to use multiple sheets of the sticky tape until most of the lint is gone. But trust me when I tell you this little trick will drastically cut down on the lint that you'll be wearing or that will infiltrate your sewing room. You'll be so tickled with the results I'm sure you'll want to write to thank me! (And please feel free to do so—I'd love to hear from you!) As my buddy, Martha, would say, "It's a good thing."

Sew!
Let's Make Jelly Roll Magic!

Prepare to be amazed at all the wonderful blocks you can create using strips and precuts. Mastering a few fundamental cutting and piecing skills to get the most out of Jelly Roll strips and precut fabric packs is easy.

You can make all the blocks in this book either using the specialty rulers designed to save time, money, and fabric, or you can make them using more traditional methods. Both methods are reviewed in detail in the Get Set chapter (pages 10–15). Let's dive right in to having fun with your fabrics!

Basic Units from Precuts

Patch	Description	How to Cut	Image
A	Quarter-square triangle (QST)	Cut triangles from 2½" strips using Side A of the EZ Flying Geese ruler OR Cut a 5¼" square twice diagonally. (You can also cut larger QSTs from Layer Cake squares.)	
B	Half-square triangle (HST)	Cut triangles from 2½" strips using Side B of the EZ Flying Geese ruler OR Cut a 2⅞" square once diagonally. (You can also cut larger HSTs from Layer Cake squares.)	
C	Square	Cut 1½" x 1½" squares from Honey Bun strips. Cut 2½" x 2½" squares from Jelly Roll strips. Charm Pack squares are 5" x 5". Layer Cake squares are 10" x 10".	
D	Rectangle	Cut 1½" x 2½" rectangles from Honey Bun strips. Cut 2½" x 4½" rectangles from Jelly Roll strips. Cut 2½" x 5" rectangles from Charm Packs. Cut 5" x 10" rectangles from Layer Cakes.	
E	Diamond	Diamond cut from 2½" strips using the 45-degree line and 2½" markings on the EZ Jelly Roll Ruler OR rotary ruler.	
F	TRI triangle	Triangle cut from 2½" fabric strip using TRI tool OR using template (page 90).	
G	RECS triangle	Triangle cut from 2½" fabric strip using the RECS tool OR using template (page 90).	

Constructing Basic Block Units

Description	Construction	Pieced Unit
Half-square triangle unit	Place two HSTs right sides together and stitch on the long side. Press seam allowance toward darker triangle OR Use the traditional method (page 11).	
TRI-RECS unit	Sew RECS triangles to either side of a TRI unit. Press the seam allowances away from TRI unit.	
Rectangle unit	Sew two rectangles together. Press the seam allowance toward the darker rectangle.	
Four-Patch unit	Sew two squares together. Press the seam allowance toward darker squares. Make two units; flip one unit, place RST, and sew. Press the seam allowance to one side, or press the seam open so unit lies flat.	
Rectangle-Squares unit	Sew two squares together. Press the seam allowance toward the darker square. Sew a rectangle to the two-squares unit. Press the seam allowance toward the rectangle.	
Flying Geese unit	Sew a B (side triangle) to an A (center triangle), matching notched edge to notched edge and pointed edge to pointed edge. Press the seam allowance toward the wing. Sew a second B triangle to other side of A triangle and press as before. OR Use the traditional method (page 12).	

Triple-Triangle unit	Sew two QSTs together along the short sides. Press seam allowance toward darker triangle. Sew a HST to the QST unit on long side. Press the seam allowance toward the HST.	
Stem unit	Cut 1 rectangle 1¼" x 5½". Cut a 2½" x 2½" square once diagonally. Sew the rectangle between the 2 triangles. Press the seam allowances toward the rectangle. Trim the ends and square-up.	
Quad-Triangle unit	Use contrasting Honey Bun strips or cut a 1½" wide strip from contrasting Jelly Roll strips. Use Side A of EZ Flying Geese ruler to cut QSTs. Sew two contrasting Side A triangles together along the short sides. Press the seam allowance toward the darker triangle. Make 2 units, alternating the placement of the fabrics. Place them RST and sew. Press the seam allowance open so unit lies flat. OR Use 4 triangles from contrasting 3¼" x 3¼" squares, cut twice diagonally.	
Triangle-Triangle unit	Sew two QSTs to the sides of a HST unit on the short side. Press seams away from the HST. Sew a large HST to this unit. Press the seam allowance toward large triangle.	
RECS Rectangle units	Sew 2 RECS triangles together. Make 2 units. Join the 2 RECS units to form a square. Press the seam allowance toward darker fabric.	

PRESTO!
LET'S SEW

Dazzling quilts go together like magic.

Amazing! All you need are a few basic ingredients such as strips, squares, and triangles and you end up with fabulous quilts in a jiffy!

Dazzling Diamonds

Quilting with Jelly Rolls opened up an entire new world of design opportunities for me. I reveled in the ability to cut squares, rectangles, and triangles from those highly versatile 2½" strips. But after awhile my mind began to wander to what else I could do with strips that was a bit more "out of the box."

Cutting diamonds from Jelly Rolls wasn't the first thought to pop into my mind, but once I realized all the wonderful possibilities of diamond units, my mind was set on fire with endless ideas! By constructing Lone Stars without those pesky set-in seams, I discovered that squares made from two diamond wedges could be rotated in a number of different ways to achieve a wide variety of design settings—each of them equally stunning! The hard part for you as it was for me is choosing which setting to use. Simply employ your design wall or an obliging floor to sample all the different layouts you can create using Jelly Roll diamonds!

JELLY ROLL LONE STAR MAGIC!

Cutting Diamonds from Strips

Line up the 45-degree line of a rotary ruler along the bottom edge of your fabric strip and trim the edge triangle.

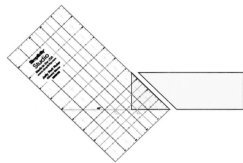

Slide the ruler over to the cutting line that matches the width of a fabric strip (in the case of a Jelly Roll strip, the 2½" line). Cut the diamond shape.

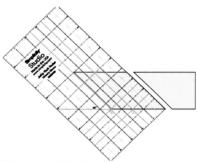

Making Diamond Units

Make a strip-set with fabric #1 & #2 and a second strip-set with fabric #2 & #3.

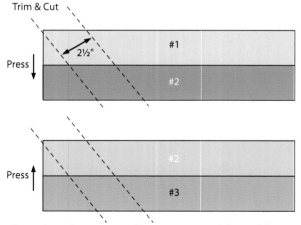

Press the strip-set seam allowances toward the #2 fabric strip.

Align the 45-degree line on the ruler with the bottom edge of the strip-set, trim the end, then cut diamond segments 2½" wide.

Cut 8 segments from each strip-set.

Sew 1 segment from each strip-set together to make diamond wedge units. Make 8 for each Lone Star.

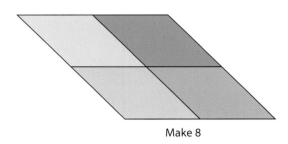

Make 8

Constructing the Lone Star WITHOUT Set-In Seams

Cut 4 – 5" background fabric squares once diagonally to yield 8 triangles (A).

Sew the A triangles to the diamond wedge units as shown.

Press the seam allowance toward the background fabric triangles.

Cut 4 – 6⅝" background fabric squares once diagonally to yield 8 triangles (B).

Sew the B triangles to the diamond wedge units.

Press the seam allowance toward the background fabric triangle.

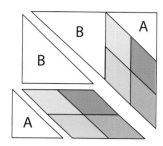

Sew 2 wedges together to form squares. Press the seams open.

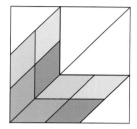

Carefully trim the excess background fabric if necessary.

Join the squares to form the Lone Star block. Press the seams open.

Square up the block if necessary.

Log onto my website at **www.kimberlyeinmo.com** for a photo tutorial of how to expertly piece a Lone Star block using no set-in seams!

Constructing the Lone Star WITH Set-In Seams

Make the diamond wedge units as before.

Join in pairs, join the pairs, and join the halves to complete the center star.

Cut 4 – 4½" Side A triangles.

Add to the sides of the center star unit using Y-seam construction.

Press the seam allowance toward the background squares.

Cut 4 – 6¼" x 6¼" squares of background fabric.

Add to the corners using Y-seam construction. Press the seam allowance toward the background squares.

Kimberly's Top Tip

Here's the bottom line on Jelly Roll Lone Stars: Depending on a variety of factors including individual ¼" seams allowances, thread weight and needle size, the brand of sewing machine, and plain old-fashioned cutting accuracy, everyone's star will end up measuring somewhere between 19" and 20½" unfinished. Don't stress!

My stars consistently end up 20" unfinished, which means I need to adjust the next border to compensate for being short by half an inch. If your Lone Star ends up measuring less than 20½" unfinished, you will need to compensate before you can add the next border or row of blocks. Simply add an inner border of a different fabric or add background fabric strips of the width necessary to make your unfinished block measure 20½" (or larger). Or in the case of LONE STARBURST (page 24), simply make all your blocks consistently the same size. No one will know once the blocks are sewn togther in the quilt!

LONE STARBURST

65" x 65", made by the author, quilted by Birgit Schüller

Block size: 10" x 10"   Skill level: Intermediate

Get Ready...

Cutting instructions are written for use with EZ Jelly Roll Ruler.

FABRIC	YARDAGE	CUTTING INSTRUCTIONS
1 Jelly Roll or 40 – 2½" strips	2½ yards	Divide strips into groups of lights, mediums, and darks. Pair up 10 groups of 4 strips each (see below for further instructions). Cut 288 single diamonds OR cut 144 diamond pairs from strip units.
Background	3 yards	Cut 5 – 5" strips; subcut 36 – 5" squares. Cut each square once diagonally to yield 72 A triangles. Cut 6 – 6⅝" strips; subcut 36 – 6⅝" x 6⅝" squares. Cut each square once diagonally to yield 72 B triangles. Cut 8 – 3½" strips from length of fabric for outside borders.
Backing	4¼ yards	Cut 2 panels 36" x 73".
Binding	¾ yard	Cut 8 – 2¼" strips for the binding.
Batting		73" x 73"

Get Set…

Kimberly's Top Tip

The trick to using 40 different strips to make Lone Stars is this: You'll need 2 very similar strips to construct the middle "radiant" row (#2) that contrast with the fabrics you select for the center and outer points of the star.

Sort your strips into groups as follows: star point row #1 = 1 strip; radiant row #2 = 2 strips (similar in scale and color); inner star #3 = 1 strip. You'll need 10 groups of 4 strips each.

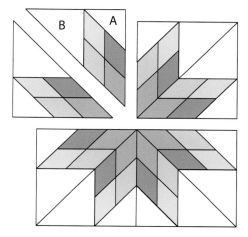

Use two fabric strips of similar color, value, and scale for the radiant row (#2). They will "read" like the same fabric when used in your stars.

Group your fabric strips in sets of 4 strips each with high contrast between the two #2 fabrics and the #1 & #3 fabrics.

Sew!

Sew a fabric #1 and #2 strip-set; and sew a fabric #2 and #3 strip-set. Press seams toward the #2 strips.

Cut 8 diamonds in 2½" widths from each strip-set.

Sew the diamond units together to make 8 diamond pairs.

Piece blocks with 2 diamond wedges and 4 background triangles (see pages 22–23). Make 36.

Blocks should measure 10½" unfinished. Square-up if necessary.

Arrange the blocks in 6 rows of 6 blocks each as shown. Try one of the many different possible arrangements or create your own layout!

Add a border of 3" wide background fabric strips.

Baste, quilt, bind, add a label, and enjoy.

Quilt assembly

Thoughts About the Quilting

The center star and partial stars were each quilted in the ditch. Then all the diamonds in each star were quilted with a variation of a swirl design. The arrangement of the stars in the quilt top and the "feel" of the fabrics could best be complemented and accentuated by a traditional-yet-sweet motif; hence, the addition of the hearts. A heart shape was quilted in the setting squares of the center Star block and repeated in each setting square area around the remaining stars – 68 of them to be exact!

Freehand feathers quilted in a traditional style were the perfect accompaniment to the hearts and give the quilt a balanced, lovely look. Freehand hearts and more feathers were added in this fashion in the outer background fabric areas near the binding.

Try This! Just for fun, select an alternate layout.

Each design uses the same 36 blocks

CHECKERBORDER RAINBOW STAR

24" x 24", made by the author, quilted by Birgit Schüller

Skill level: Confident beginner

Get Ready...

Cutting instructions are written for use with the EZ Jelly Roll Ruler.

FABRIC	YARDAGE	CUTTING INSTRUCTIONS
1 Jelly Roll or 32 – 2½" strips	2½ yards	Keep the strips in order as they come off the roll. Choose 32 of the 40 strips and set aside 8 for use in another project. Assign each strip a number from 1 to 32, and make a chart to keep them organized.
Background	⅓ yard	Cut 1 – 6⅝" strip; subcut 4 – 6⅝" x 6⅝" squares and cut each square once diagonally to yield 8 triangles. Cut 1 – 5" strip; subcut 4 – 5" x 5" squares and cut each square once diagonally to yield 8 triangles.
Binding	⅜ yard	Cut 4 – 2¼" strips.
Backing	1 yard	Cut 1 square 30" x 30".
Batting		30" x 30"

Get Set…

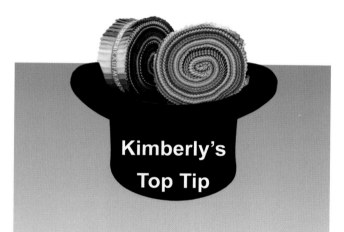

Kimberly's Top Tip

When working with rainbow strips, you will cut single diamonds from the strips rather than cutting 2-diamond units from strip-sets, as the illustrated instructions show (page 22). It isn't difficult to construct a Lone Star from single diamonds, but you'll want to take your time and pay careful attention to the number chart (page 30).

I recommend viewing the chart as a clock. Begin from the 12 o'clock position, then assemble each four-diamond wedge and piece your way in a clockwise direction. Straight pins will come in very handy for pinning seams and matching points.

Use the 45-degree line on the EZ Jelly Roll Ruler and cut 1 – 2½" diamond from each of 32 rainbow-colored strips for the center star.

Lay out your strips in order as you cut.

Cut 3 – 2½" x 2½" squares from each of the 32 rainbow-colored strips for the checkerboard border. Label all your cut pieces by number.

While I was cutting my diamonds and squares, I cut triangles, too, because I knew I'd want them for another project. (See Lovely Little Leftovers, pages 80–83.)

Piece the Lone Star and add the background fabric triangles (see pages 22–23), following the placement chart below.

Lay out the star diamonds before you begin stitching to check the placement. Work in a clockwise direction around the star.

If necessary, add background fabric strips around the center medallion block so the unfinished star measures 20½" x 20½".

Following the color placement chart, make the side borders with 10 two-patch units each and add to the quilt.

Following the color placement chart, make the top and bottom borders with 14 two-patch units each and add to the quilt.

Baste, quilt, bind, add a label, and enjoy!

Thoughts About the Quilting

This colorful top was the perfect place to use a set of machine quilting melon guides by Kim Brunner (see Resources, page 94). The tone-on-tone batik fabrics allowed more quilting details to show and this was taken into consideration when the quilting was planned. First, the outside of the star was quilted in the ditch followed by four radiating melon shapes quilted in the center, filling in the sections around them.

The eight star points were quilted one at a time. In the outer-most diamond of each star point, a curved line was quilted to the tip and a mirrored line was quilted back to form a narrow oval that was then filled with a string of pebbles. Freehand feathers were the perfect choice in the background setting squares and triangles. In order to continue the melon theme from the star into the checkerboard border, overlapping spaces were created then filled with more feather designs. A narrow oval with pebble fill quilting from the star tips was used again in the four corners of the border.

Color placement chart

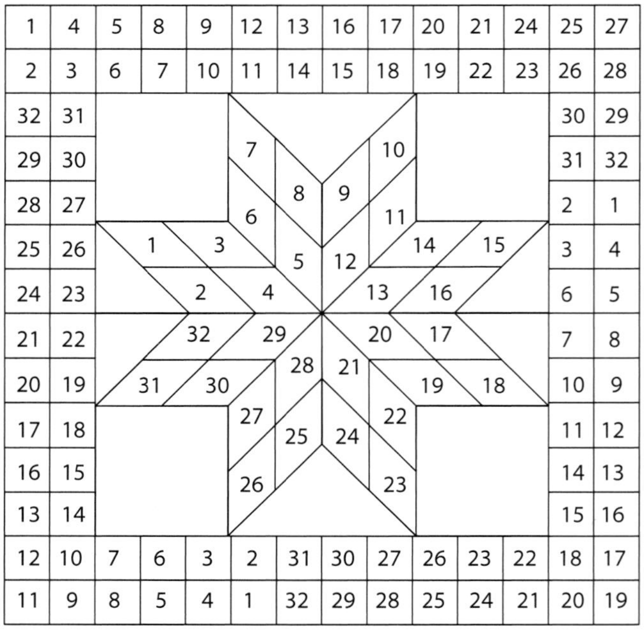
1 4 5 8 9 12 13 16 17 20 21 24 25 27
2 3 6 7 10 11 14 15 18 19 22 23 26 28
32 31 30 29
29 30 31 32
28 27 2 1
25 26 3 4
24 23 6 5
21 22 7 8
20 19 10 9
17 18 11 12
16 15 14 13
13 14 15 16
12 10 7 6 3 2 31 30 27 26 23 22 18 17
11 9 8 5 4 1 32 29 28 25 24 21 20 19
7 10 8 9 6 11 1 3 5 12 14 15 2 4 13 16 32 29 20 17 28 21 31 30 19 18 27 22 25 24 26 23

RADIANT RAINBOWS

You can find them in almost every quilt store you enter these days from almost every fabric manufacturer. Rainbow-colored bundles are just waiting for someone to unlock a powerhouse of hidden design potential! I can't begin to tell you the number of times I've been asked by friends and students alike: "I think rainbow strip bundles are beautiful, but how do you use them effectively in a quilt?"

Although these delectable textile tidbits are enticing, most quilters simply don't know what to do with them or how to use them effectively. Admittedly, using a rainbow pack of strips can be rather daunting, but never fear! The real beauty of these color-wheel strips is that the fabric manufacturers have already done the work of putting those strips in the order of the color wheel for you. All you have to do is keep them in order and cut them up. It's quilting almost like painting by numbers!

So the next time you see a bundle of rainbow strips and they seem to be calling your name, go ahead and indulge! I'll show you how to use them to their best advantage and you'll love the results. And your friends will be amazed at your expert application of color theory. (Sounds super impressive, but it's super easy to do!)

RAINBOW GEESE CROSSING

56" x 56", made by the author, quilted by Birgit Schüller

Block size: 7" x 7"   Skill level: Intermediate

Get Ready...
Cutting instructions are written for use with EZ Flying Geese ruler.

FABRIC	YARDAGE	CUTTING INSTRUCTIONS
1 Jelly Roll or 40 – 2½" strips	2½ yards	Use Side A of EZ Flying Geese ruler to cut 3 triangles (geese units) from each of 40 different strips.
Background Fabric	2½ yards	Cut 6 – 5¼" strips; subcut strips into 40 – 5¼" x 5¼" squares. Cut the squares once diagonally to yield 80 triangles. Cut 10 – 2½" strips. Fold strips RST; use Side B of EZ Flying Geese ruler to cut 120 pairs of triangles (120 wing units). Cut 4 – 7½" x 42" strips for the outer borders.
Fabric #1—Paisley Print (includes binding)	¾ yard	Cut 3 – 2½" strips; use Side A of EZ Flying Geese ruler to cut 36 triangles. Cut 6 – 2¼" strips for the binding.
Fabric #2—Blue	¼ yard	Cut 3 – 2½" strips; use Side A of EZ Flying Geese ruler to cut 44 triangles.
Backing	3¾ yards	Cut 2 panels 32" x 64".
Batting		64" x 64"

Get Set...

Kimberly's Top Tip

The work of arranging your strips into a rainbow effect has been done for you by the fabric manufacturer. Once you open your Jelly Roll bundle, label them from 1 to 40 and keep your strips in order as you cut. If you are using strips from your own stash, use a color wheel as a guide to arrange them.

I recommend piecing one block at a time to keep your pieces and blocks straight. Trust me when I tell you it is very easy to get confused if you jump ahead or try to chain piece all the Flying Geese at the same time!

Sew!

Use 3 each of 40 different colors to make a total of 120 Flying Geese units (see pages 11–12). Label each unit with the "goose" fabric number

Join 3 Flying Geese units and press the seam allowances as shown. Follow the numbered placement diagram (page 34) to sequence the Flying Geese units in each block.

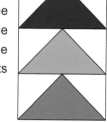

Make 40 units of 3 Flying Geese each.

Add a background fabric triangle to the sides of the triple Flying Geese unit and press away from the geese.

Add the fabric #1 and #2 triangles (check placement carefully!) and press seam allowances as before. Make 40 blocks.

The blocks should measure 7½" x 7½" unfinished. Square-up if necessary. Leave ¼" seam allowances at the points.

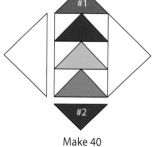

Make 40

Rainbow Geese Crossing

Lay out the blocks according to the numbered placement diagram below. Join the blocks into 9 four-block units. Use pins to match points when joining the blocks.

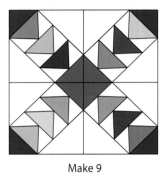

Make 9

Press the seams open.

The four-block units should measure 14½" square unfinished. Square-up if necessary. Set aside 4 three-geese units for the border corners.

Join the units into rows and join the rows together. Add the border and corner blocks. Baste, quilt, bind, add a label, and enjoy!

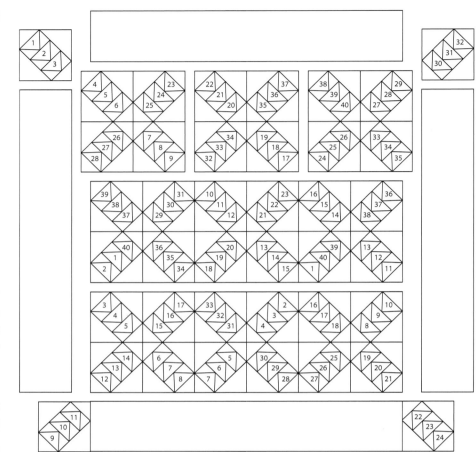

Placement diagram

Thoughts About the Quilting

Flying Geese blocks are absolutely one of the best (and most fun) blocks to machine quilt! This top has a very geometric setting with the direction of the geese changing within each block. Quilted straight lines originate from the tip of the center triangle in each Flying Geese unit. The colorful squares created by four triangles coming together at the corners made a square "target" and were the perfect place to add interesting shapes and curves. Freehand feathers were the perfect complement for the border portion of the background in order to add some "whimsy" to go with the bright and colorful paisley fabric in the corners and binding.

Try This! Essential tools to unleash your inner design diva

While it's easy and efficient to make quilts from published patterns and books, I'd like to encourage quilters of all skill levels to nurture their own inner creative goddess while learning to design their own original quilts. It's easier than you think!

Here are a few handy tools and tips to get you started:

Quilt design software: I have used Electric Quilt® software since version 3 and love it! (The current version is 7). The interface is extremely user friendly and I find the software is very intuitive when it comes to various block settings, adding new fabrics, and customizing sizes. Design software will even calculate yardage amounts and print rotary-cutting directions or templates. The software gives you a sneak peek at your quilt on the computer screen before you commit the fabric.

Graph paper, pencil, and ruler: Even though I use computer design software, I still keep these simple implements handy. They have been serving aspiring artists well for decades. You can work out a myriad of mathematical problems with a ruler and compass. Take time to learn some basic drafting skills and you can draft any block to any size. My own personal preference? I like to use a mechanical pencil whenever possible, but a #2 yellow pencil with a sharp point (keep a sharpener handy) works perfectly well, too.

Calculator: You'll need to do the math to figure out just how many units to cut and how much fabric to buy. It doesn't take a fancy calculator, but you'll definitely need one that works properly.

Quilt block reference materials: Look for design software such as EQ's BlockBase or quilt block reference books in your local library. An Internet search engine is also a great way to research the names of published quilt blocks.

Internet: There are so many websites dedicated to quilting it can be mind-boggling. A recent unofficial search of the word "quilting" brought up over 16 million hits! The Internet is a great resource for design ideas. Browse through quilters' blogs, online shops, and search using key words. Refine your search and you'll find a thousand ideas to inspire you to create unique and original quilts.

Digital camera: There is probably no better inspiration anywhere than the world around you. Whether you are a seasoned traveler or never leave town, there is inspiration to behold around every corner. Be ready to capture design inspiration by carrying a compact point-and-shoot digital camera wherever you go. When inspiration strikes, you'll be ready to capture it digitally for future reference.

Books and magazines: You probably have stacks of books and magazines lying around you haven't looked through in years. Even if you don't, I'm sure your friends have periodicals they would be willing to let you peruse. Your local quilt guild may have a lending library of books and reference materials. Whenever I need to recharge my creative mojo, I find browsing through some quilt magazines always gets my mind revved up and ready to go.

Start small: If you've never designed an original quilt before, don't become overwhelmed by thinking you have to design your own personal magnum opus right up front. Start with a small, doable project. For example, sampler quilts are a great way to make a unique and personal quilt using simple settings. By choosing your favorite blocks and pretty fabrics you'll have a quilt as unique as your own fingerprint when you're finished.

Everyday inspiration: Keep your ears and eyes open for inspiration all around you. There are ideas galore if you'll allow yourself to be open to them. Observe your kids or grandkids, talk to friends, go window shopping, sort through your old UFOs, or even clean your sewing room! Just open your mind to new ideas and let them flow. Pick an idea or topic you're interested in pursuing and get moving. You'll find that momentum will carry you along and you'll gain confidence in your own design skills the more you stretch them.

Spinning Spools

64" x 82", made by Carla Conner, quilted by Birgit Schüller

Block size: 8" x 8"   Skill level: Confident beginner

Get Ready...

Cutting instructions are written for use with EZ Flying Geese ruler.

FABRIC	YARDAGE	CUTTING INSTRUCTIONS
1 Jelly Roll or 40 – 2½" strips	2½ yards	The pieces for each block should be cut from the same Jelly Roll strip: Cut 2 – 2½" x 2½" squares (96 total). Use Side B of the EZ Flying Geese ruler to cut 6 triangles (288 total).
Background	3 yards	Cut 8 – 2½" strips; use Side B of the EZ Flying Geese ruler to cut 192 triangles. Cut 12 – 2½" strips; subcut 192 – 2½" x 2½" squares. Cut 12 – 2½" strips; use Side B of EZ Flying Geese ruler to cut 288 triangles.
Border	2½ yards	Cut 8 – 2½" strips; use Side B of the EZ Flying Geese ruler to cut 192 triangles. Cut 7 – 5½" strips for the border.
Binding	¾ yard	Cut 8 – 2¼" strips.
Backing	5 yards	Cut 2 panels 35" x 90".
Batting		72" x 90"

Get Set…

Kimberly's Top Tip

You only need 24 Jelly Roll strips to cut the triangles and squares for the Spool blocks. There is more than enough fabric in one strip to cut units for at least 2 blocks. Sort through your strips and set aside any that are too light in color and value or where the scale of print is too large to work well in these blocks. Save them for another project.

Sew!

Pair the Jelly Roll Side B triangles with background triangles to make 6 HSTs for each block (total 288).

Pair background and border fabric triangles to make 192 HSTs.

Make 192

Make 6 for each block (total 288)

HSTs should measure 2½" x 2½" unfinished. Square-up if necessary.

Assemble each Spool block with 6 squares and 10 HSTs.

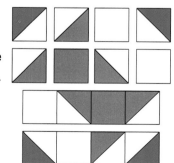

Blocks should measure 8½" square unfinished. Square-up if necessary.

Make 48

Spinning Spools

Arrange the blocks in 8 rows of 6 blocks each, alternating the orientation of the blocks to achieve the spinning layout.

Add the border.

Quilt, bind, add a label, and enjoy.

Quilt assembly

Thoughts About the Quilting

This quilt has three distinct areas—the spools, the background, and the border. First, the blocks were stitched in the ditch around each spool. Background areas were filled in with quilting. Since the blocks are uniform, visual interest was created by adding quilting in positive and negative areas. Some small sections were left without quilting to add dimension and texture. The direction of freehand feathers was alternated and a set of circle guides was used to achieve circular lines around the center squares. Freehand feathers were quilted in each spool, which allowed the stitching to travel conveniently from one spool to the next.

To add excitement to the rather plain border, each was divided into logical units and curved guides were used to fill them with geometric shapes resembling Gothic cathedral windows, which were echo quilted several times. The overall result is stunning and the perfect complement to the simple shapes that accentuate the radiant rainbow colors!

Jelly Roll Seasons

Browse through any quilt shop these days and the selection of fabrics seems practically endless as those creative folks who design for the fabric manufacturers keep coming up with beautiful new fabric lines we just can't seem to resist! But have you noticed? There are all sorts of seasonal and holiday fabrics available that are just perfect for making quilts and accent pieces to add to your home décor throughout the year!

Now you can find many of those scrumptious holiday and seasonal fabrics all wrapped up in precut bundles! All the seasons and holidays are represented— spring, summer, autumn, and winter, Christmas, Halloween, Valentine's Day, etc. As each season approaches I am simply enthralled with all the new seasonal colors and delightful print options that entice me to add more things to my "must make" list. I just adore decorating our home for the seasons and the holidays. So here are four fun projects just perfect for using a seasonally themed fabric bundle. The bonus is that each of these cinch-to-stitch designs will look just as pretty if you choose to make them with non-seasonal fabrics with a planned fabric palette.

One more thing: for the TRY THIS! suggestions in some of the projects in this chapter, I direct you to some seasonal, family-tested, tried-and-true recipes. I hope you'll give them a try and discover how easy and delicious they are to make. Your family and friends will love them and you'll enjoy having a bit of extra time for quilting while enhancing your quilting lifestyle!

Have you ever noticed that once you untie the bow on the strips in a Jelly Roll they all seem to explode? You'll never be able to roll them back up again—not that this is a bad thing!

Spring Fling

48" x 48", made by Claire Neal, quilted by Birgit Schüller

Block Size: 12" x 12"   Skill level: Intermediate

This quilt may look complicated, but it's actually one big Nine-Patch made up of 9 Nine-Patch blocks!

Get Ready...

Cutting instructions are written for use with the EZ Jelly Roll Ruler and the EZ Flying Geese ruler.

FABRIC	YARDAGE	CUTTING INSTRUCTIONS
1 Jelly Roll or 40 – 2½" strips	2½ yards	Divide strips into piles of LIGHTS, MEDIUMS, MEDIUM DARKS, and DARKS. From each of 5 DARK strips, cut 4 – 2½" x 2½" squares (20 total). Fold the remaining 5 DARK strips RST and use Side B of the EZ Flying Geese ruler to cut 4 PAIRS of triangles (wings) for the Spring Star blocks Flying Geese units. Cut 20 – 2½" x 2½" squares from LIGHT strips. Cut 16 – 2½" x 4½" rectangles from LIGHT strips. From each of 4 MEDIUM strips, cut 4 – 2½" Side A triangles (geese) for the May Day block Flying Geese units. From each of 4 MEDIUM strips, cut 4 – 2½" x 2½" squares (16 total). From MEDIUM-DARK strips with fabric RSU, use Side B to cut a variety of 72 triangles. From LIGHT strips with fabric RSD, use Side B to cut a variety of 36 triangles. From MEDIUM-DARK strips with fabric RSU, use Side B to cut 36 triangles.
Background	1½ yards	Cut 5 – 2½" strips; set aside for the inner border. Cut 3 – 2½" strips; subcut 20 – 2½" x 4½" rectangles. Cut 2 – 2½" strips. Use Side A to cut 20 side A triangles (geese) for the Spring Star blocks Flying Geese units. Cut 2 – 2½" strips. Fold strips RST; use Side B to cut 16 PAIRS of triangles (wings) for the May Day blocks Flying Geese units. Cut 5 – 2½" strips. Turn strips all RSD. Cut 72 Side B triangles. Cut 1 – 4½" strip; subcut 4 – 4½" x 4½" squares.
Border options	¾ yard for traditional border OR 1 Jelly Roll & scraps or Charm Squares for Piano Key border	Traditional outer border: Cut 5 – 5 ½" strips. Piano Key outer border: Cut 80 – 2½" x 4½" rectangles and 4 cornerstone squares 4½" x 4½".
Binding	¾ yard	Cut 6 – 2¼" strips.
Backing	3¼ yards	Cut 2 panels 28" x 56".
Batting		56" x 56"

Get Set…

Kimberly's Top Tip

Sort your Jelly Roll strips into piles of LIGHTS, ME-DIUMS, MEDIUM DARKS, and DARKS. Don't stress about how many strips end up in each value pile. Just try to distribute them as evenly as possible. Then relax. Have fun putting these blocks together and you'll be amazed at how your quilt will turn out!

Sew!

Spring Star Blocks

Use 4 matching 2½" x 2½" squares from each of the 5 DARK strips to make 5 four-patch units.

Make 5

For each block make 4 matching Flying Geese units with background fabric geese and DARK fabric wings. The Flying Geese units should measure 2½" x 4½" unfinished.

Add a 2½" x 4½" background rectangle to the geese side of each unit. Make 20 units.

Make 72 – 2½" x 2½" MEDIUM-DARK/ background HSTs.

Make 20

Make 36 LIGHT/MEDIUM-DARK HSTs.

For each block, make 4 corner units, each with 1 LIGHT/MEDIUM-DARK HST, 2 MEDIUM-DARK/background HSTs, and 1 LIGHT square (20 corner units total).

Make 20

Set aside the remaining 48 HSTs for the May Day blocks.

Assemble the 5 Spring Star blocks with the four-patch, Flying Geese, and corner units, matching the four-patch and wing fabrics. The blocks should measure 12½" x 12½". Square up if necessary. Make 5 Spring Star blocks.

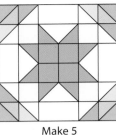

Make 5

May Day Blocks

For each block, make 4 matching Flying Geese units with MEDIUM geese triangles and background fabric triangle wings (16 total).

Add a LIGHT 2½" x 4½" rectangle to the wings side of each Flying Geese unit.

Make 16

For each block, make 4 corner units, each with 1 LIGHT/ MEDIUM-DARK HST, 2 MEDIUM-DARK/background HSTs, and 1 MEDIUM square (16 total corner units).

HSTs should measure 2½" x 2½" unfinished. Square-up if necessary.

Make 16

Assemble each May Day block with a 4½" x 4½" background square, 4 matching Flying Geese units, and 4 corner units. Blocks should measure 12½" x 12½" unfinished. Square-up if necessary. Make 4 May Day blocks.

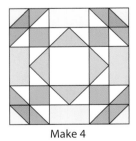

Make 4

Arrange the blocks in a Nine-Patch configuration. Sew the blocks into rows and sew the rows together.

Add the inner border, piecing the strips as necessary.

Border Options

For the Piano Key border:

Make 4 border units by joining 20 – 2½" x 4½" rectangles.

Add 2 units to the sides of the quilt.

Add 2 cornerstones to the remaining units and add to the top and bottom of the quilt.

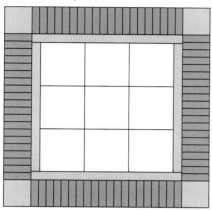

Quilt assembly with Piano Key border

For the traditional border:

Piece the 5 – 5½" strips as needed and add to the quilt.

Quilt, bind, add a label, and enjoy.

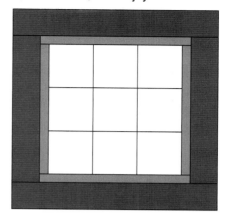

Quilt assembly with traditional border

Log on to **www.Kimberlyeinmo.com** for additonal layout options for SPRING FLING, plus my favoirte casserole for spring: Baked Spaghetti!

Thoughts About the Quilting

The romantic feel of the SPRING FLING fabrics created a whimsical and feathery mood that was enhanced by feather patterns in different arrangements in various areas of the quilt. The same pattern was used repeatedly in the same sections of each block thus creating a certain "rhythm" and preventing the impression that the quilting was random. The inner border seemed to call for some straightness – like rationalism to surround all the sweetness within. Beaming rays were used in a small amount, followed by more whimsy and lightness in the outer border. Perfectly harmonized, perfectly balanced!

An alternate colorway is shown in DELECTABLE DELIGHTS, 48" x 48", made by the author, quilted by Carolyn Archer. Because the fabrics themselves are so busy (accentuated by the busy small-scale print of the background fabric), an all-over pattern was used. Based on the name and feel of the fabric line used, A Breath of Avignon, the quilting design chosen included a variation of the familiar French fleur de lis. You can see the quilting in the outer border quite well, but because the blocks are very busy in both design and fabric prints, the quilting does manage to add much texture.

SUMMER SPARKLERS

54" x 70", designed by the author, made by Birgit Schüller   Block size: 8" x 8"   Skill level: Advanced.

It is important to refer to the quilt photograph frequently when working on this quilt.
Fabric placement is important to achieve the somewhat structured secondary design.

Get Ready...

Cutting instructions are written for use with EZ Flying Geese ruler and the EZ Jelly Roll Ruler.

FABRIC	YARDAGE	CUTTING INSTRUCTIONS
2 Jelly Rolls OR 80 – 2½" strips OR 1 Jelly Roll plus 1 Layer Cake (40 – 2½" strips plus 40 – 10" squares) (NOTE: If you use one Jelly Roll plus one Layer Cake, cut all patches from the Jelly Roll strips first and any additional patches from the Layer Cake squares.)	5 yards	Separate strips into four color groups: LIGHTS—background for Pinwheel and Twister blocks MEDIUMS (reds)—for the Twister blocks MEDIUM-DARKS (medium blues)—for Pinwheel block corner squares and Twister block centers DARKS (dark blues)—for Pinwheel blocks From each of 17 LIGHT fabrics cut: 4 – 2½" x 4½" rectangles (68 total) 4 – 2½" x 2½" squares (68 total) 12 – Side B triangles cut with fabric RSU (204 total) From 4 LIGHT fabrics cut: 1 – 2½" x 2½" square (4 total) 2 – Side B triangles cut with fabric RSU (8 total) From MEDIUM (red) fabrics cut: 17 sets of 8 – Side B triangles cut with fabric RSD (136 total) From MEDIUM-DARK (medium blue) fabrics cut: 17 sets of 4 – Side B triangles cut with fabric RSU (68 total) From 4 MEDIUM-DARK (medium blue) fabrics cut: 18 – 2½" x 2½" squares (72 total). Be sure to use 4 different squares in each Pinwheel block. From DARK blue fabrics cut: 18 sets of 8 Side B triangles cut with fabric RSD (144 total)
Inner Border	⅓ yard	Cut 6 – 1¼" strips for the inner border from 3 dark blue strips from the Jelly Roll and cut lengthwise.
Backing	4½ yards	Cut 2 panels 31" x 78".
Binding	½ yard	Cut 8 – 2¼" strips for the binding.
Batting		62" x 78"

Get Set...

Kimberly's Top Tip

Although this quilt is very scrappy, it is helpful to use MEDIUM-DARK and DARK fabrics from the same strip within each Pinwheel and Twister block. This will have a "calming" effect, with the quilt looking planned and the secondary design easier to see.

However, I recommend using a random variety of fabrics for the corner squares of the Pinwheel blocks. Be careful to choose 2½" squares that are light in value for the placement in the corners! I find it is especially helpful to assemble one block at a time to avoid confusion while you piece.

Sew!

Twister Blocks

Make Twister blocks with one red, one medium blue, and one light fabric each, matching the triangles and rectangles within each block.

For each block:
Make 4 red/medium blue HST. Press the seam allowance toward the blue triangles on 2 HST and toward the red on 2 HST.

Make 4 red/light HST. Press the seam allowance toward the red triangles.

Join the red/medium blue HST and red/light HST in pairs.

Add a light rectangle to each pair on the side of the light triangle. Press the seam allowance toward the rectangle.

Join these units in pairs, then join the 2 halves to complete the block.

Repeat these steps to make 17 blocks. The blocks should measure 8½" x 8½" unfinished. Square-up if necessary.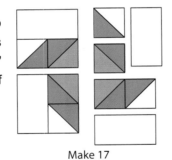

Make 17

Pinwheel Blocks

Pay close attention! Look at the photo of the quilt (page 44) and see how the background fabrics in the Twister blocks are carried into the adjacent Pinwheel blocks.

Lay out the finished Twister blocks on your design surface (or floor). Alternate the finished blocks with sets of 8 DARK (dark blue) triangles for the Pinwheel blocks.

Stack the remaining light patches onto the Twister blocks, matching the light fabrics. Then distribute a 2½" x 2½" square and 2 Side B triangles to the sides of the adjacent Pinwheel block triangle sets.

Use the remaining patches to fill in the outside edges of the corner Pinwheel blocks.

Make one Pinwheel block at a time so that the background fabrics will line up properly.

For each block:
Make 8 – 2½" HSTs. Press the seam allowance toward the blue.

Make 144

Lay out the HSTs with the MEDIUM (medium blue) and LIGHT squares according to the block diagram, matching the light fabrics with the light fabrics in the adjacent Twister blocks.

Join the HSTs and squares into rows and join the rows to complete the block.

Repeat these steps to make 18 Pinwheel blocks. The blocks should measure 8½" x 8½" unfinished. Square-up if necessary.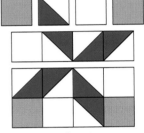

Make 18

Arrange the blocks according to the assembly diagram (page 48), being careful to maintain the alignment of the background fabrics of the Twister and Pinwheel blocks.

Sew the blocks into rows and join the rows. Press the seams toward the Pinwheel blocks. You may have to change direction based on how the seams naturally want to lie. Be flexible, and remember: steam is your friend when used judiciously!

Add an inner border using the 1¼" wide strips.

Jelly Roll Chevron Border

This fun piecing method makes a unique and captivating border treatment that looks terrific not only on the Summer Sparklers quilt, but on many other types of quilts as well.

Each border has a small Pinwheel block in the center.

Cut 16 Side B triangles from DARK blue strips with the fabrics RSD and 16 from MEDIUM red strips with fabrics RSU (32 total).

Make 16 – 2½" MEDIUM/DARK (red/dark blue) HSTs and join to make 4 – 4½" x 4½" Pinwheel blocks for the borders.

For the chevrons, cut a total of 34 matching pairs of 2½" x 10" rectangles of assorted LIGHT, MEDIUM, MEDIUM-DARK, and DARK fabrics (68 rectangles total).

Each of these 10" strip pairs must be cut on a 45-degree angle in a way that results in 2 large and 2 small patches.

Use the templates (page 90) or the rulers as described below.

Place 2 (2½" x 10") matching rectangles RST.

Align the 2" line on the EZ Jelly Roll Ruler with the left end of the rectangles. Then place Side B of the EZ Flying Geese ruler against the right edge of the Jelly Roll Ruler as shown.

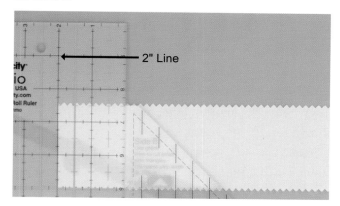

Hold the EZ Flying Geese ruler in place, remove the Jelly Roll ruler, and cut along the 45-degree edge.

Flip back the top rectangle and make 2 pairs of large and small chevron patches as follows: Combine the large patch from the top strip (B1) with the small patch of the bottom strip (A2). Combine the small patch of the top strip (A1) with the large patch of the bottom strip (B2).

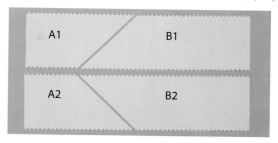

Repeat with the remaining 33 matching pairs of rectangles. Sort the chevron pairs into two piles according to the angle of the cut on the larger patches. You'll have 2 piles of 34 pairs of chevrons in each pile each.

For the top and bottom borders you need 1 small Pinwheel block and 14 chevron patch pairs. Make sure the 45-degree cut is in the same direction on all the large patches for one border and in the opposite direction on the second border.

For each of the side borders you need 1 small Pinwheel block and 20 chevron patch pairs. Again, the angle on the large patches should be in one direction on one border and in the opposite direction on the second border.

Position the small Pinwheel block on point. Add a chevron patch pair to 2 sides of the block, adding the shorter patch first, then the longer patch.

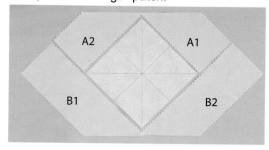

Add 7 chevron pairs to each side of the Pinwheel block for the top and bottom borders, always adding the shorter patch first.

Add 10 chevron pairs to each side of the Pinwheel blocks for each side border.

Trim the borders to measure 6¼" wide. Make sure to leave a ¼" seam allowance on the small Pinwheel block at the top and bottom corners!

Top & bottom borders Make 2
Side borders Make 2

Add the borders to the quilt in the same way that you would add a mitered border.

Mark a dot ¼" inside all 4 corners of the quilt top and at the inside angled corner on each of the borders.

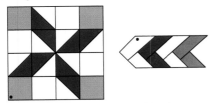

Mark ¼" inside the quilt top and border corners.

Add the 4 borders, matching the point of the Pinwheel block with the center of each side and pinning at the marked dots at the corners. Be careful not to stretch the bias edges.

Start and stop sewing at the dots, leaving the ¼" seam allowance open.

Sew the seam at each corner from the outside edge in toward the quilt top, again stopping at the dots. Press the seam allowances open.

Piece the corner blocks.

Join 4 – 2½" wide scraps as shown. The longer scraps should be at least 5" long and the short scraps at least 3" long. Make 4 scrap sets.

Cut a triangle from each using Side A of the EZ Flying Geese ruler, aligning the 4½" line with the edge of the longer scraps.

Cutting the corner triangles

◄— 4½" line

Cut 4 triangles and add them to the corners of the quilt top.

As the border patches are cut on the bias, I recommend that you stay-stitch around the outer edges of the quilt top ⅛" from the edge to avoid stretching while handling or quilting it.

Baste, quilt, bind, add a label, and enjoy!

Quilt assembly

Try This!
Crock Pot Pulled Pork Barbeque is my favorite summer easy-fix meal.

Anyone who knows me knows I'm a slow-cooker magician! I love to combine all the ingredients in the crock pot in the morning and let them simmer all day, leaving time for stitching or a thousand other summer pastimes. This tasty recipe is a real crowd pleaser and is perfect for soccer game picnics or for dinner by the pool, lake, or campsite. Simply log onto www.kimberlyeinmo.com and download the recipe for this delicious, stick-to-your-ribs summer fare. And don't forget to have some creamy coleslaw on hand!

Thoughts About the Quilting

This festive and patriotic quilt called for a similar style of quilting to accentuate the feel of summer sparklers and firecrackers. Continuous curves were added to the outside of the pinwheels to achieve the impression of movement and wind with continuous oval spirals within each of the pinwheel blades.

The background areas were filled with pebble quilting—perfect for a summery beach or lake-side theme. A tight braided rope was quilted in the narrow inner border to give the quilt a nautical feel. Continuous swirls were added to the outer pieced chevron border to balance all the designs.

LEAVES IN THE PUMPKIN PATCH

54" x 54", made by the author, quilted by Birgit Schüller

Block size: 6" x 6"   Skill level: Confident beginner

Get Ready...

Cutting instructions are written for use with EZ Flying Geese ruler and the EZ Jelly Roll Ruler.

FABRIC	YARDAGE	CUTTING INSTRUCTIONS
1 Jelly Roll OR 40 – 2½" strips	2½ yards	Select 24 strips and cut enough pieces from each strip to make 2 blocks OR cut enough for 2 blocks from 8 strips and one block from the remaining 32 strips for a total of 48 Leaf blocks. Instructions are for cutting pieces for one block. Cut 1 – 2½" x 2½" square. Cut 1 – 2½" x 4½" rectangle. Use Side B to cut 4 triangles RSU. After cutting all the leaf pieces, cut the pieces for the border. Cut 4 – 2½" x 2½" squares for the cornerstones. Use Side B to cut a variety of 100 triangles RSU.
Background	3 yards	Cut 3 – 2½" strips; subcut 48 – 2½" x 2½" squares. Cut 8 – 2½" strips: use Side B to cut 192 triangles with the strips RSD. Pair with the leaf triangles to make 192 HST units (4 matching units for each Leaf block). Cut 3 – 2½" strips; subcut 48 – 2½" x 2½" squares. Cut the squares once diagonally for the stem units. Cut 4 – 2½" strips; use Side B to cut 100 triangles with the strips RSD. Pair with the Side B triangles cut from Jelly Roll strips RSU to make 100 HST units for the outer border. Cut 7 – 6½" strips; subcut 16 – 6½" x 6½" squares.
Brown (stem fabric)	⅓ yard	Cut 2 – 5½" strips; subcut 48 – 1¼" x 5½" rectangles.
Inner Border	¾ yard	Cut 6 – 1¼" strips for the inner border strips. Cut 6 – 2¼" strips for the binding.
Backing	3¾ yards	Cut 2 panels 31" x 62".
Batting		62" x 62"

Get Set...

Kimberly's Top Tip

These fun little blocks fly together like falling leaves on a blustery day. (I just love the imagery of that mental picture. It reminds me of that classic *Winnie the Pooh* cartoon!) Don't worry if some of your prints are large in scale. You may have to fussy-cut units from your strips, but use them anyway. The large-scale prints will add visual interest, dimension, and excitement to your quilt. Throw caution to the wind!

Sew!

For each Leaf block, use 4 RSD Side B background fabric triangles and 4 RSU Jelly Roll fabric triangles to make 4 – HST units 2½" x 2½" (192 total).

Press the seam allowances toward the Jelly Roll fabric triangles.

Make an additional 100 HSTs for the outer Sawtooth border.

The HST units should measure 2½" x 2½" unfinished. Square-up if necessary.

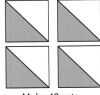

Make 48 sets
(total 192)

Make 100

Sew the 1¼" x 5½" stem fabric to a background triangle. Press the seam allowance toward the stem.

Add a second triangle to the unit and press as before.

Trim the stem unit to measure 2½" x 2½". Make 48.

Make 48
Stem units

Assemble the Leaf blocks as shown.

Blocks should measure 6½" x 6½" unfinished. Square-up if necessary.

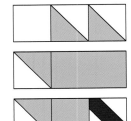

Make 48 Leaf blocks

Arrange the Leaf blocks and 16 background squares as shown being careful to rotate each Leaf block to achieve the desired layout.

Add the inner border fabric strips to the sides, top, and bottom.

Make 4 Sawtooth border units with 25 HSTs each.

Add borders to the side of the quilt.

Add a cornerstone square to the ends of the remaining border units and add to the top and bottom of the quilt.

Baste, quilt, bind, add a label, and enjoy!

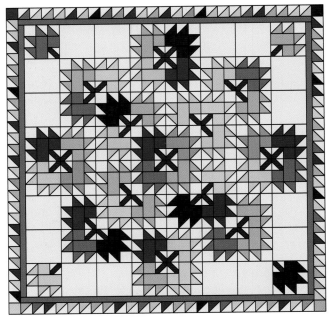

Quilt assembly

Try This! My favorite Autumn Casserole—Turkey Tetrazzini

This is pure cool-weather comfort food at its best! And when I serve this dish (which is actually just as tasty with chicken instead of turkey), my family gobbles it up lickety-split. This is one of the few things I really enjoy eating as a leftover, but the truth is that there are rarely any leftovers to save for another meal. It's easy to prepare and freezes beautifully—the perfect dish to make when you need a meal for home and one to take to your church or guild potluck. Simply log on to www.kimberlyeinmo.com and download the recipe for this oh-so-tasty, ultimate comfort casserole. *Bon appétit!*

Thoughts About the Quilting

Since this traditional-style quilt shouts fall and harvest by the very nature of the Leaf blocks, the impression of movement was added through the machine quilting. As a twist, rather than stitching in the ditch around the leaves, the leaves were outlined with scribble-style quilting. Inside each Leaf block 4 swirly quilting designs were added with tight roping in the stems. While traveling from block to block, leaf designs were quilted in the medium-size sections. Pumpkin designs fill the large areas along the edges in the background fabric squares.

As a clever marking trick, Birgit used a clear sheet of plastic (like the ones for overhead projectors) and marked the outline of the area to be quilted with a dry-erase marker. At her desk, she played with different pumpkin/leaf layouts until she felt satisfied with the results. At the sewing machine, she "stitched" on the drawn lines with an unthreaded needle to make a stencil from the plastic sheets. After she carefully erased all the drawn lines, she used both sides of the plastic sheets (mirror images) to mark the quilt for the machine quilting.

Starry Pines

64" x 64", made by the author, quilted by Birgit Schüller

Block size: 8" x 8"   Skill level: Advanced

Get Ready...

Cutting instructions are written for use with EZ Flying Geese ruler and the EZ Jelly Roll Ruler.

FABRIC	YARDAGE	CUTTING INSTRUCTIONS
Jelly Rolls AND 1 Charm Pack OR 1 Layer Cake Separate into color groups of reds, greens, and light prints. You will need at least 8 green prints and 5 red prints to make this quilt as shown.	2½ yards	From 9 red strips: With the fabric RSU, cut 64 Side B triangles from 2½" strips (combine with background fabric Side B triangles to make 64 HST units). From 4 – 2½" strips; with 2 strips RST, subcut 36 pairs of Side B triangles (72 triangles total); then subcut 20 Side B triangles with the strips RSU. From 8 green strips: Cut 2 – 2½" squares from each of 8 green strips. Set aside remaining green fabric strips (or 1¼ yards of green) to make the Tree blocks. (See the cutting instructions on page 58.) From light print strips: From 2 – 2½" strips; cut 16 Side B triangles from fabric strips facing RSU. From the Charm Pack (or Layer Cake): Cut 5 – 3⅜" x 3⅜" squares from light fabrics for the square-in-a-square star centers. Cut 4 – 3⅜" x 3⅜" squares from red fabrics for the square-in-a-square star centers.
Background	2 yards	Cut 3 – 2½" strips. With fabric RSD, subcut 64 Side B triangles (to combine with red Side B triangles to make 64 HST units). Cut 3 – 2½" strips; subcut 36 Side A triangles. Cut 12 – 2½" strips; subcut 40 – 2½" x 2½" squares, 24 – 2½" x 4½" rectangles, and 12 – 2½" x 8½" rectangles. Cut 9 – 2½" strips for the first and fourth interior borders. Set remaining strips aside for Tree blocks. (See the cutting instructions on page 58.)
Green	¼ yard	Cut 4 – 1½" strips for the second interior border.
Red	¼ yard	Cut 5 – 1½" strips for the third interior border.
Backing	4¼ yards	Cut 2 panels 36" x 72".
Batting		72" x 72"
Binding	¾ yard	Cut 9 – 2¼" strips for the binding.

Get Set...

Kimberly's Top Tip
Although this quilt looks complex, it is actually not too difficult to piece if you keep your patches and units organized. I think you'll find it extremely helpful to number your red and green strips and make a legend or key to keep track of them. As you assemble the Star and Tree blocks, you'll be able to see where each fabric belongs. This clever pattern would also look beautiful using batik fabrics of icy silvers, deep greens, and frosty blues for a wintry theme.

Sew!

Flying Geese

Use 72 (36 pairs) red Side B triangles and 36 Side A background triangles to assemble Flying Geese units for Star blocks. Press the seam allowances toward the wings (side triangles).

The Flying Geese units should measure 2½" x 4½" unfinished. Square-up if necessary.

Make 36

Square-in-a-Square

Use 20 red Side B triangles and 5 – 3⅜" light squares to make 5 Square-in-a-Square units.

Use 16 light Side B triangles and 4 – 3⅜" red squares to make 4 Square-in-a-Square units.

The Square-in-a-Square units should measure 4½" x 4½" unfinished. Square-up if necessary.

Make 5   Make 4

Star Blocks

Use the Flying Geese units, Square-in-a-Square units, and 2½" x 2½" background squares to construct 9 Star blocks.

The blocks should measure 8½" x 8½". Square up if necessary.

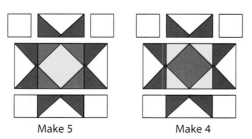

Make 5   Make 4

Half-Square Triangles

Use 64 Side B red and 64 Side B background triangles to make HST units.

Press the seam allowances toward the red triangles.

The HST units should measure 2½" x 2½" unfinished. Square-up if necessary.

Make 64

Sashing

Make 24 sashing units with 2 – 2½" x 2½" HST units and 1 – 2½" x 4½" rectangle each as shown. Pay attention to the orientation of the HSTs!

Make 24

Quilt Center

Arrange the Star blocks, 12 sashing units, and 4 – 2½" x 2½" green square cornerstones in rows. Join the rows, then sew the rows together.

Quilt center assembly

Interior Borders

Join the remaining 12 sashing units with 12 – 2½" x 8½" rectangles.

Join 12 – 2½" x 2½" green squares with 12 – 2½" x 2½" red and background HST units. Pay close attention to the orientation of the HSTs.

Join 4 – 2½" x 2½" background squares with 4 – 2½" x 2½" red and background HST units, paying close attention to their orientation.

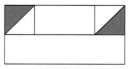

Make 12   Make 12   Make 2   Make 2

Make 4 border units as shown.

Add to the quilt.

Side Border Units
Make 2

Top and Bottom Border Units
Make 2

Add the 2½" wide background border.
Add the 1½" wide green border.
Add the 1½" wide red border.
Add the 2½" wide background border.

Quilt center assembly

Kimberly's Top Tip

Each block contains half of 2 trees and is made with 2 different tree fabrics. I strongly recommend you make one block at a time, beginning with a side block and working your way around the quilt, leaving the corner blocks until all 24 side blocks are done. That way, you'll be able to match the fabrics of each tree. Trust me—this cutting and piecing process can be very tricky, but it's well worth the effort.

Thoughts About the Quilting

Since the fabric line used to make this quilt was whimsical, a freehand scribble-style outline was quilted and a variation of a swirly design was added in all the stars. The center patches were quilted with spirals in all the small stars. A Christmas light chain design was quilted in the red and green inner border strips with the lights alternating in direction. Each tree was outline quilted in a similar style and a quilted garland was added with a festive star on top of each tree. The background quilting was also done in a less-formal, whimsical manner with meandering ribbons and bows.

Tree Blocks

Label your green fabrics #1 through #8 and track them on your fabric key.

Pay close attention to whether cuts are made with the fabrics right-side up (RSU) or right-side down (RSD). If not specified, cut RSU.

The patches are cut as follows:

From 2½" green fabric strips cut:	CUTTING METHOD
Patch #1	Use side B of the EZ Flying Geese ruler. Align the straight ruler edge with the left edge and the 2½" line with the bottom edge of your fabric strip. Cut.
Patch #2	Align the 1" line of the EZ Jelly Roll Ruler with the straight end of your 2½" fabric strip. Align Side B of the EZ Flying Geese ruler with the right edge of the EZ Jelly Roll Ruler. Cut.
Patch #3	Align the 2" line of the EZ Jelly Roll Ruler with the straight end of your fabric strip. Align Side B of the EZ Flying Geese ruler with the right edge of the EZ Jelly Roll Ruler. Cut.
From 2½" background fabric strips cut:	
Patch #4	Align the 4" line of the EZ Jelly Roll Ruler with the straight end of your fabric strip. Align Side B of the EZ Flying Geese ruler along the 2½" line with the right edge of the EZ Jelly Roll Ruler. Cut.
Patch #5	Use the EZ Flying Geese ruler to cut a 45-degree triangle from the end of your fabric strip. Align the 4" line and the 45-degree line of the EZ Jelly Roll Ruler with the diagonal edge of your fabric strip. Cut.

FABRIC	CUTTING INSTRUCTIONS
Trees	Select 2 – 2½" strips each of fabrics #1, #5, #6, and #8; subcut each into 3 - #1, #2, and #3 patches RSD and 3 - #1, #2, and #3 patches RSU. Select 2 – 2½" strips each of fabrics #2, #3, #4, and #7; subcut each into 4 - #1, #2, and #3 patches RSU and 4 - #1, #2, and #3 RSD.
Background	Cut 7 – 2½" strips; subcut into 24 - #4 patches RSU and 24 - #4 patches RSD. Cut 7 – 2½" strips; subcut 24 - #5 patches RSU and 24 - #5 patches RSD. Subcut 4 – #1, #2, and #3 patches RSU and 8 – #1 and 4 – #2 patches RSD. Cut 1 – 4½" strip; subcut into 4 – 4½" squares and 4 – 2½" squares.

There are three variations of the Tree blocks. You will need to pay close attention to the placement of the fabrics used in each block. Adjust the layout depending on the number of green fabrics you have in your Jelly Roll or stash of strips.

For Block A, use tree patches cut RSD and background patches cut RSU. (Numbers shown here refer to patch #s.)

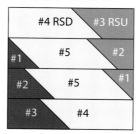
Block A – Make 12

For Block B (which is a mirror image of Block A), use tree patches cut RSU and background patches cut RSD.

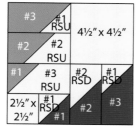
Block B – Make 12

For Block C (the corner blocks), you'll need tree and background patches cut both RSU and RSD. Refer to the chart to the left.

Block C – Make 4

Make the Tree blocks as shown and press the seam allowances toward the green fabrics. The numbers shown in the chart below refer to the sequence of green fabrics.

The blocks should measure 8½" x 8½" unfinished. Square-up if necessary.

Assemble the blocks for the outer border, alternating the Tree blocks A and B as needed to achieve the design.

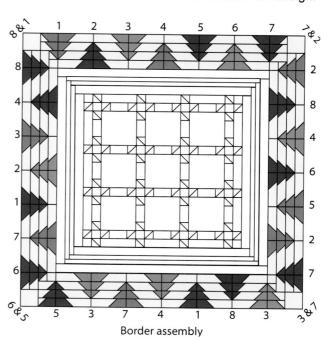
Border assembly

Try This!
Fond memories and giggles of a sticky, green treat—Christmas Holly

Indulge me while I reminisce a little. While in college, right before the winter break, my best friend and roommate, Beth, told me about a tasty treat called "holly" she and her mother made every year. I talked her into showing me how to make it. Since we didn't have a car, we snuck the ingredients out of the dining hall and went back to the rec room in our dorm. I'll never forget how we melted mini-marshmallows, butter, and green food coloring in a beat up old bowl in the microwave. Then we added a couple of cereal bowls full of corn flakes.

Now, you have to get a mental picture of this. I think we had one spoon between the two of us but somehow we ended up mixing these ingredients with our

hands as we tried to drop small globs on a cafeteria tray to make the holly. Let me just say there was green goo everywhere except where it was supposed to be! I honestly don't think I've ever laughed so hard in my life!

I took that recipe home to my mom that year and we started the tradition of making holly every year. (It worked out much better in a kitchen setting.)

You can log onto **www.kimberlyeinmo.com** and download the recipe. It is similar to those crispy rice treats we all know and love, but instead you end up with a fun little confection that looks absolutely merry on a plate full of Christmas cookies! I hope you'll try it. Ho ho ho!

EXTRA EASY APPLIQUÉ

The funny thing about quilting with Jelly Roll strips and precuts is that they are often overlooked when it comes to using them with appliqué techniques. I say, au contraire! There are so many options for incorporating quick and easy machine appliqué, which opens up an entirely new avenue of creative possibilities. Even the most dedicated piecers can enjoy a change from their usual stitching pace to employ fusible web and a hot iron. It's quick, super-simple, and offers even more ways to channel your creativity.

Many of you own machines that do all sorts of fabulous decorative stitching. Even basic machines feature zigzag and buttonhole stitches. I like to use this analogy: our sewing machines are like our brains—we tend to use only 10% of their capability! Machine appliqué using precuts is a chance to switch gears from your perfect ¼" piecing stitch and try out some of those whimsical stitches on your machines. Gather those nifty decorative threads you've wanted to try and get sewing! And for all you piecing fun-atics out there, you'll still have the thrill of stitching your blocks together but with a renewed sense of accomplishment after you try some of these machine appliqué treats!

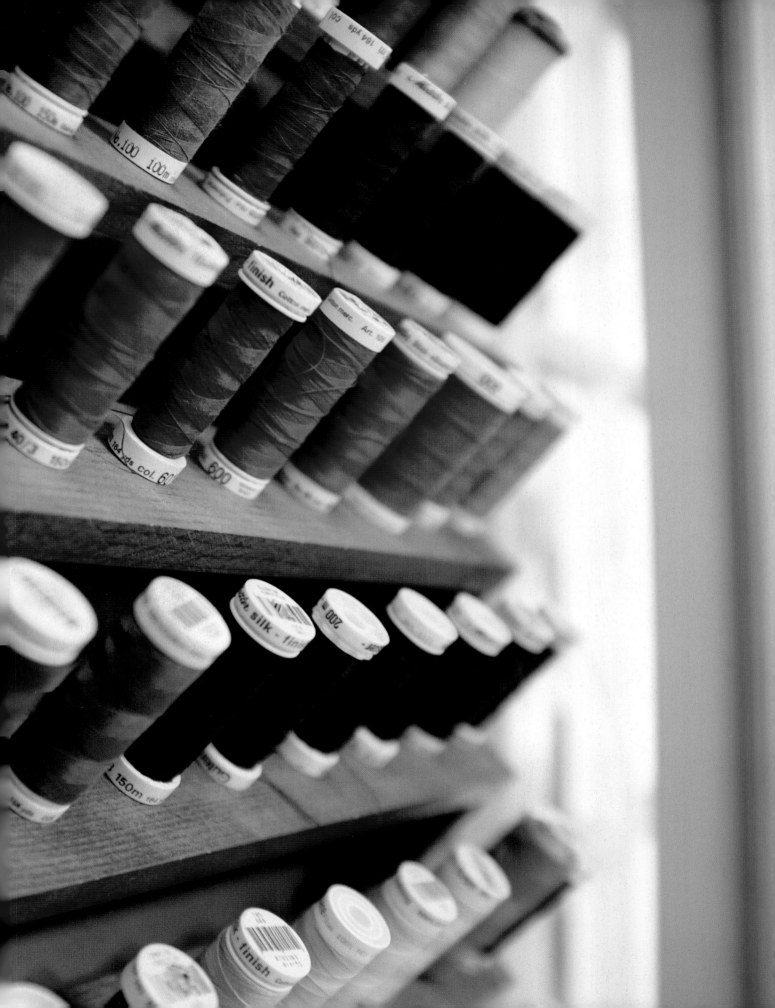

Just Dotty

58" x 72", made by the author, quilted by Carolyn Archer
Block size: 10" x 10"   Skill level: Skilled Beginner

Get Ready...

Cutting instructions are written for use with the EZ Jelly Roll Ruler and the Easy Circle Cut tool (optional).

FABRIC	YARDAGE	CUTTING INSTRUCTIONS
1 Jelly Roll Plus 1 Layer Cake OR 2 Layer Cakes You will need at least 12 pieces 10" square or larger.	5 yards	Set aside 12 – 10" Layer Cake squares for the large circles. Cut 320 – 2½" x 2½" squares from the Jelly Roll strips or Layer Cake squares.
Background	3 yards	Cut 3 – 10½" strips; subcut 12 – 10½" x 10½" squares. Cut 4 – 6½" strips; subcut 20 – 6½" x 6½" squares. Cut 2 – 15⅜" strips; subcut 4 – 15⅜" x 15⅜" squares. Cut the squares twice on the diagonal to yield 16 side setting triangles (you will only need 14). Use the remaining fabric to cut 2 – 8" squares. Cut the squares once on the diagonal to yield 4 corner setting triangles.
Fusible Web	3 yards	Buy it on a roll, rather than folded in a package, if possible.
Tear-away Stabilizer	3 yards	To use beneath the machine-appliquéd circles.
Backing	4⅔ yards	Cut 2 panels 33" x 80".
Batting		66" x 80"
Binding	½ yard	Cut 7 – 2¼" strips.

Kimberly's Top Tip

To cut the appliqué circles using the Easy Circle Cut tool, simply fuse the back of each fabric square with fusible web, just as you would if you were using the templates. Fold the fused squares in half, paper side out. Line up the folded edge on the appropriate fold line on the acrylic tool and cut with an 18mm rotary cutter.

Additional supplies:

EZ Circle Cut Tool or circle templates (page 91)
3 yards lightweight fusible web
3 yards tear-away stabilizer
Neutral thread for piecing
Contrasting thread for decorative appliqué stitching (See Try This! page 65.)

Get Set...

Begin by removing any fabrics that are too close in value and hue to the background fabric, especially if your background fabric is from the same line as your Jelly Roll or Layer Cake fabrics.

Sew!

Fuse stabilizer to the backs of 12 different 10" squares. Cut 12 – 7½" circles using template #1 (page 91) OR the 7" line on the EZ Circle Cut tool. (The tool includes a ¼" seam allowance, so the 7" line results in a 7½" circle.)

Fuse the circles to 12 – 10½" x 10½" background squares.

Position tear-away stabilizer beneath the squares and use your favorite stitch to machine appliqué the circles in place to complete the Circle blocks.

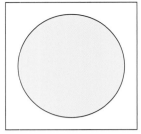

Make 12 Circle blocks

For the Bordered Circle blocks, fuse stabilizer to the backs of 20 – 10" squares.

Cut 20 circles using template #2 (page 91) OR the 3" line on the tool.

Fuse the circles to 20 – 6½" x 6½" background squares.

Position tear-away stabilizer beneath the squares and machine appliqué the circles in place.

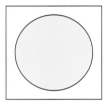

Make 20

Kimberly's Top Tip

Trust me when I tell you to always, always use tear-away (temporary) stabilizer underneath the blocks when you do any machine-appliqué technique. If you don't, your fabric will pull and pucker and your pieces won't lie flat or look pretty. It is worth the extra effort to use the stabilizer and your blocks will be beautiful! Be sure to remove the stabilier carefuly after stitching in place.

Make the pieced rectangle units: Sew 3 – 2½" x 2½" squares together. Press all the seam allowances in one direction. Make 40.

Make 40 3-square units.

Sew 5 – 2½" x 2½" squares together. Press all the seam allowances in one direction. Make 40 .

Make 40 5-square units.

Make 20 blocks by adding the 3-square units to the top and bottom of the 20 – 6½" x 6½" background/circle units, then adding the 5-square units to the sides. Press the seams away from the background fabric after each addition.

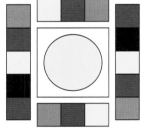

Make 20
Bordered Circle blocks

For the setting triangles, fuse stabilizer to enough of the remaining fabrics to cut 18 circles using template #3 (page 91) or the 2" line on the tool.

Fuse to the backs of the side and corner setting background fabric triangles.

Position tear-away stabilizer beneath the squares and machine appliqué the circles in place.

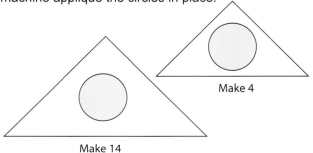

Make 4

Make 14

Remove the tear-away stabilizer from all the machine appliquéd circles.

Arrange the blocks and setting triangles in diagonal rows.

Sew the blocks and triangles into rows, then join the rows to complete the top.

Baste, quilt, bind, add a label, and enjoy!

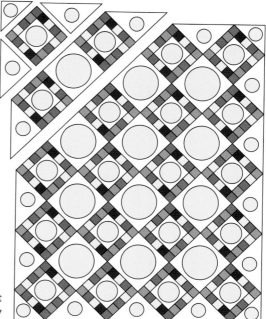

Quilt assembly

Thoughts About the Quilting

This quilt has a sleek, contemporary vibe and the machine quilting needed to complement this modern element. The background fabric squares behind the circles were quilted with a close, freehand wavy stripe pattern that accentuates the circles and gives them dimension. The circles were each quilted with a stylized flower motif that balanced the quilting across the surface but still allowed the circles to "pop" off the background squares. To keep the quilt from becoming too serious, individual swirls were quilted in each of the 2" squares surrounding the medium circles, which added movement and flow to this dynamic quilt.

Try This!
Twice the Pizzazz—
Double needle machine-appliqué technique.

Just look at the difference! Even the most basic decorative stitches made with a single needle become dazzling simply by using a double needle instead! I made a test sample using several different utility stitches—first with a single needle, then with a size 4.0 double needle and some variegated decorative cotton thread. The results were quite unexpected and amazing!

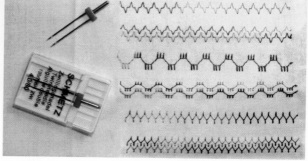

You'll never know what those stitches will look like with a double needle until you try them. The circles on this quilt are the perfect place to showcase those fancy decorative stitches using this technique. It makes ordinary machine appliqué extraordinary and so is much more fun than simply doing invisible machine appliqué. Spend an afternoon experimenting using different stitches, threads, and stitch widths and just have fun!

Faux Cathedral Windows

This quilt is quick and easy whether you make the Layer Cake (large) version or the Charm Pack (small) version. It's a great way for you to learn to do fusible machine appliqué and hone your skills.

Layer Cake version:
70" x 70", made by the author, quilted by Carolyn Archer, Ohio Star Quilting
Block size: 9½" x 9½"
Skill level: Skilled Beginner

Charm Pack version:
34" x 34", designed by the author, made by Christie LaCroix, Quilt Patch Deco Quilting
Block size: 4½" x 4½"
Skill level: Skilled Beginner

Get Ready...

Layer Cake Version

FABRIC	YARDAGE	CUTTING INSTRUCTIONS
1 Layer Cake	2½ yards	Choose 36 – 10" squares for the block centers.
White Print for appliqué	2 yards	Use Template #1 (page 70) to trace the appliqué shapes onto the paper side of the fusible web. Fuse to the back of the fabric. Trace and cut out 80 appliqué pieces.
Navy Blue for appliqué	1¾ yards	Use Template #1 to trace the appliqué shapes onto the paper side of the fusible web. Fuse to the back of the fabric. Trace and cut out 64 appliqué pieces.
Inner Border and Binding	⅞ yard	Cut 6 – 2" strips for the inner borders. Cut 7 – 2¼" strips for the binding.
Outer Border	2 yards	Cut 4 – 6" strips LOF for the outer border.
Backing	4⅝ yards	Cut 2 panels 39" x 78".
Batting		78" x 78"

Charm Pack Version

FABRIC	YARDAGE	CUTTING INSTRUCTIONS
1 Charm Pack	1½ yards	Choose 36 – 5" squares for the block centers.
Aqua Print for appliqué	½ yard	Use Template #2 (page 70) to trace the appliqué shapes onto the paper side of the fusible web. Fuse to the back of the fabric. Trace and cut out 48 appliqué pieces.
Rust Print for appliqué and Binding	¾ yard	Use Template #2 to trace the appliqué shapes onto the paper side of the fusible web. Fuse to the back of the fabric. Trace and cut out 72 appliqué pieces. Cut 4 – 2¼" strips for the binding.
Brown Print for appliqué and Border	¾ yard	Use Template #2 to trace the appliqué shapes onto the paper side of the fusible web. Trace and cut out 24 appliqué pieces. Cut 4 – 3½" strips for the border.
Backing	1¼ yards	Cut 1 panel 42" x 42".
Batting		42" x 42"

ADDITIONAL SUPPLIES	LAYER CAKE VERSION	CHARM PACK VERSION
Fusible Web	3 yards	1½ yards
Tear-away Stabilizer	3 yards	1½ yards

Get Set...

Kimberly's Top Tip

Be sure to use good quality fusible web. I prefer the "lite" weight. Once fused, the appliqué pieces are soft and easy to stitch. If the fusible web you have on hand is old and brittle, toss it out and buy new, from a bolt or roll if possible. It will save you endless hours of frustration and a sticky mess on the soleplate of your iron.

You must use tear-away (temporary) stabilizer underneath your blocks when you stitch over the raw edges of the appliqué pieces. Don't skip this ultra-important step of using stabilizer; you'll be disappointed with the rumply results if you do.

If your precuts have "pinked" edges, leave just a smidgeon of those edges showing when you fuse your appliqué arc. The uneven edges will be buried in the seam allowance later on.

Sew the Layer Cake Version!

Lay out the arcs on the 10" x 10" squares as shown. Following the manufacturer's instruction, fuse the arcs in place.

Make 8

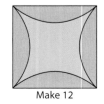
Make 12

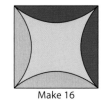
Make 16

Using your favorite stitch and machine appliqué technique, stitch the arc pieces to the squares. I used a basic satin stitch with a high-contrasting (red) thread to make the arcs really stand out.

Lay out the blocks in rows as shown.

Join the blocks into rows and join the rows. Press the seams open to reduce the thickness and make your blocks lie flat.

Add the borders.

Baste, quilt, bind, add a label, and enjoy.

Quilt assembly

Sew the Charm Pack Version!

Lay out the arcs on the 5" x 5" squares as shown. Following the manufacturer's instruction, fuse the arcs in place.

Make 4   Make 16   Make 16

Lay out the blocks in rows as shown.

Join the blocks into rows and join the rows. Press the seams open to reduce the thickness and make your blocks lie flat.

Add the borders. Baste, quilt, bind, add a label, and enjoy!

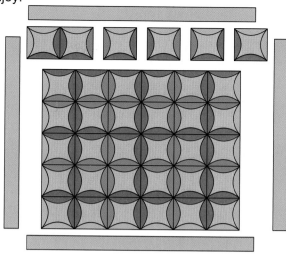

Quilt assembly

Thoughts About the Quilting

Using the precut squares as "backgrounds" for each block created an interesting and challenging canvas for the machine quilting.

On the Layer Cake version, an allover pantograph design was a better choice than custom quilting because customized motifs would have stood out conspicuously on the squares with fabrics that read like a solid but blended in on fabrics with busy prints. The appliquéd arcs are the real stars of these blocks and quilting was used to created subliminal dimension and texture.

On the Charm Pack version, feather motifs were quilted in each square and a fun, freehand squiggle design was quilted in the arcs to create lots of visual interest. The quilting on both quilts is equally effective and compliments the block layouts perfectly!

Try This! Use Charm Pack squares to make yo-yos!

Have you seen those fabulous plastic disc yo-yo makers? (See Resources, pages 93–94.) These ingenious, nifty notions are incredibly easy to use, so much fun, and highly addictive! I keep a little basket with my yo-yo makers, charm squares, scissors, needles, and thread handy and ready to go whenever I have a few minutes to sit and do some hand stitching. I've made hundreds of yo-yos on long car trips up and down I-75, while I'm watching TV with the guys, or even while I'm chatting with friends on the phone. (Talk about being a master multi-tasker!)

Of course you can make yo-yos from charm squares the old fashioned way, but I'd like to encourage you to give these gadgets a try and rediscover these versatile little fabric gems for making quilts, crafts, garlands, and other accessories.

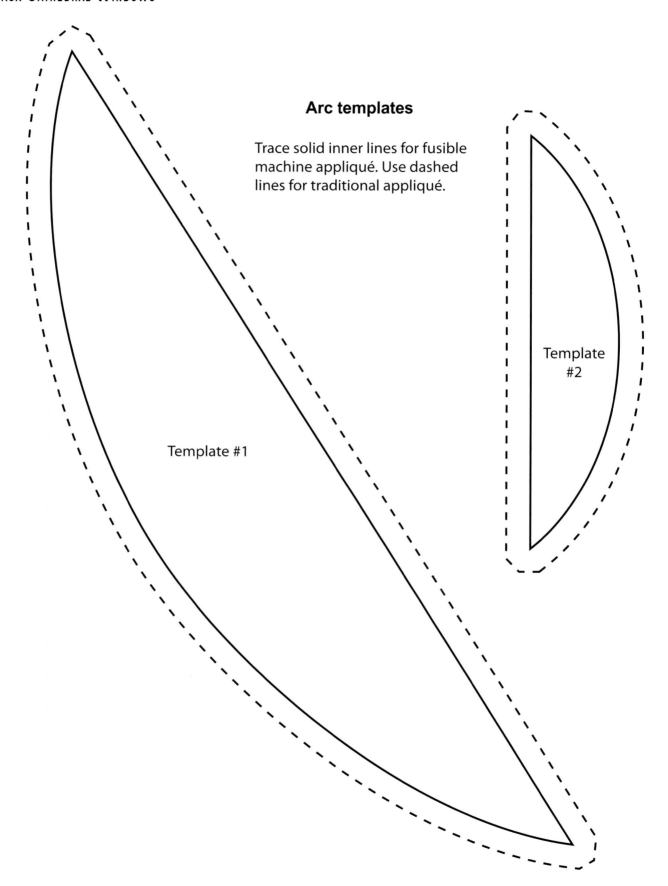

Arc templates

Trace solid inner lines for fusible machine appliqué. Use dashed lines for traditional appliqué.

Template #1

Template #2

FABULOUS FUN—FAST AND DONE!

I believe we all need to laugh more and stress less. Quilting is our happy place, our color therapy, our stress reliever. We all need to lighten up, have more fun, and not take things too seriously. Even in quilting, mistakes sometimes happen to the best of us—in fact, right underneath the eyes of quilting professionals, as you'll see on page 76. (Can you spot the block that is turned incorrectly? Three of us worked on that quilt and we didn't spot the error until it was already quilted!) My point is, don't let the small things in life get you down or stress you out. Just laugh and move on.

So put some great tunes on your iPod, listen to an audio book, or watch your favorite movie on DVD while you stitch. (May I suggest a comedy?) Unwind. Decompress. Let the worries of the world slip away while you enjoy some much needed (and well deserved) sewing time and color therapy. And don't forget to laugh at least once a day. You know the kind—a good, hearty, from-the-bottom-of-your-gut laugh. Remember: a merry heart doeth good like a medicine. Wise words!

STICKS & STONES

78" x 86", designed by the author; made by Judy Schrader, Glendale, Arizona;
quilted by Carolyn Archer, Ohio Star Quiltilng
Block size: 8" x 8"   Skill level: Beginner

Get Ready...

Cutting Instructions are written for use with EZ Jelly Roll Ruler.

FABRIC	YARDAGE	CUTTING INSTRUCTIONS
2 Jelly Rolls OR 1 Jelly Roll plus 1 Layer Cake OR 80 – 2½" strips	5 yards	Separate the fabrics into 5 color groups. Assign each color group a number from #1 to #5. Cut 28 – 2½" x 4½" (B patches) from a variety of strips from each of the 5 color groups (144 total). Cut 28 – 2½" x 6½" (C patches) from a variety of strips from each of the 5 color groups (144 total).
Light	1½ yards	Cut 9 – 2½" strips for the four-patch units Cut 9 – 2½" strips; subcut 144 – 2½" x 2½" squares (A patches).
Contrasting Fabric (red)	¾ yard	Cut 9 – 2½" strips for the four-patch units.
Inner Border	⅔ yard	Cut 8 – 2½" strips.
Outer Border	2½ yards	Cut 4 – 5½" strips from LOF.
Backing	5½ yards	2 panels 43" x 94".
Batting		86" x 94"
Binding	¾ yard	Cut 9 – 2¼" strips.

Get Set…

Other than separating your strips into five different color groups, don't work too hard trying to make your blocks "matchy-matchy." A scrappier version is much more visually interesting.

Sew!

Make 9 strip-sets with the LIGHT and CONTRASTING 2½" fabric strips. (Do not use your Jelly Roll strips for this step.) See the figures on page 74.

Rotate one strip-set and place RST on top of another strip-set, butting the seams together and matching opposite fabrics. Cut into 16 – 2½" segments, keeping strip units RST.

Repeat 3 times with 6 of the remaining strip-sets.

Cut the 9th strip-set in half, position the halves RST, and cut 8 – 2½" segments.

Cut a total of 72 segment pairs.

Sew the segment pairs together along one edge; press each unit closed, then press the seam to one side. Make a total of 72 four-patch units.

Get Set…

Kimberly's Top Tip

When feeding your four-patch units underneath your presser foot, make sure the seam allowance on the top segment is facing away from you (toward the presser foot). While this might seem like it would be more difficult, your presser foot will push your seams to "snuggle" together and ensure perfect points in the center. It works like magic every time!

The four-patch units should measure 4½" x 4½" unfinished. Square-up if necessary.

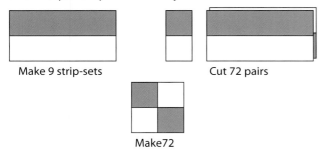

Make 9 strip-sets   Cut 72 pairs

Make72

Select 2 A patches (light squares) and 2 each B & C patches (rectangles) from the same color group.

Sew an A patch to the end of a B and C patch.

Make a block by adding to the four-patch unit in the following order: the B patch, A/B patch, C patch, and A/C

patch. Press the seams away from the four-patch unit after each addition.

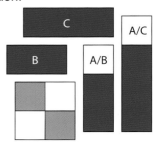

Block Assembly

Repeat these steps, making the number of blocks shown for each color group.

> Make 14 color group #1 blocks.
> Make 14 color group #2 blocks.
> Make 15 color group #3 blocks.
> Make 15 color group #4 blocks.
> Make 14 color group #5 blocks.

Thoughts About the Quilting

The geometric design of this quilt is so dynamic that a lot of custom quilting isn't necessary and might actually be wasted because it wouldn't show. A fun, stylized all-over quilting design was chosen that complements the whimsical and vibrant fabric line perfectly.

If you decide to quilt this on a domestic sewing machine, consider turning the quilt upside down and quilting it from the back side up. You won't be distracted by the seams, fabrics or busy pattern of the blocks and you can concentrate on keeping your free-motion stitches evenly spaced and balanced. It's the perfect way to improve your quilting skills!

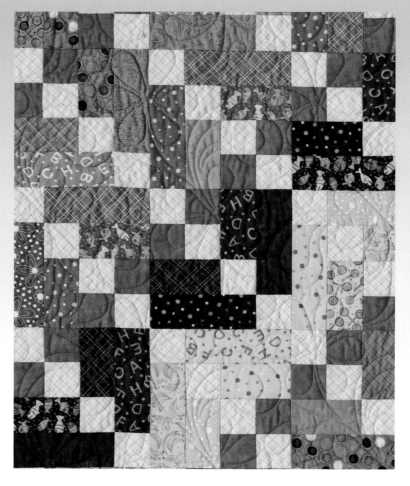

Blocks should measure 8½" x 8½" unfinished. Square-up each block if necessary.

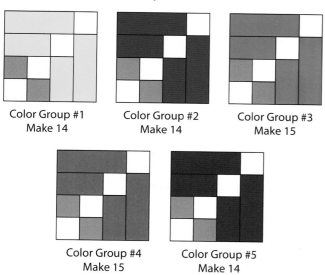

Color Group #1
Make 14

Color Group #2
Make 14

Color Group #3
Make 15

Color Group #4
Make 15

Color Group #5
Make 14

Arrange the blocks in rows, being careful to rotate each block to achieve the diagonal pattern of the contrasting fabric in the four-patch units.

Sew the blocks into rows and join the rows.

Add the inner and outer borders.

Baste, quilt, bind, add a label, and enjoy!

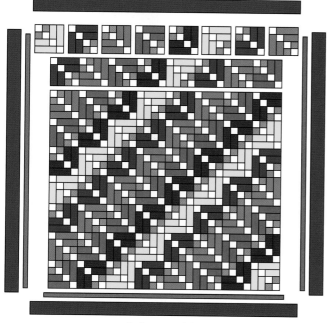

Quilt assembly

Try This! When in doubt, here's what to buy.

How many times has this happened to you? You've been out shopping at your favorite quilt shop or on a shop hop with friends and you've spied the most wonderful Jelly Roll or precut fabric bundle. It practically calls your name from across the room! (I know, it happens to me all the time.) But at the time, you're either in the middle of working on another project or you simply don't have a specific project in mind for this gorgeous new precut bundle of fabrics in the perfect shade of loveliness. Oh my…what to do?

Here's a great rule of thumb that will allow you to buy the yardage you need to make just about any mid-size quilt. Along with the irresistible Jelly Roll (or Layer Cake) purchase:

- 1½ yards for background fabric
- 1½ yards of contrasting fabric for an inner border and binding
- 1½ yards for an outer border
- And for a little extra insurance, buy 1 matching Charm Pack!

SHOOTING STARS

80" x 80", designed by the author, made by Ilona Baumhofer, quilted by Birgit Schüller
Block size: 8" x 8"   Skill level: Intermediate

Psst! So what if there's an itty bitty mistake in this quilt? If this happened to you, what would you do? Would you stress out, get upset, rip it all out, and change it? Or would you say, "It's absolutely beautiful just the way it is!" I chose the latter. Quilting is much more fun when everything doesn't always have to be perfect. Let go and enjoy!

Get Ready...

Cutting Instructions are written for use with EZ Flying Geese ruler and EZ Jelly Roll Ruler.

FABRIC	YARDAGE	CUTTING INSTRUCTIONS
1 Jelly Roll	2½ yards	Cut 4 rectangles 2½" x 4½" from each of 16 strips (total 64). Cut 4 side B triangles from the same 16 strips (total 64).
1 Layer Cake	2½ yards	Separate your Layer Cake squares by values of at least 8 LIGHTS, 16 MEDIUMS, and 8 DARKS OR into 3 distinct color groups. Choose 32 – 10" squares; trim to measure 9" x 9". Cut each 9" square once diagonally to yield 2 triangles. Set aside 1 each of 32 triangles.
Background	2½ yards	Cut 4 – 9" strips; subcut into 16 – 9" squares. Cut squares once diagonally to yield 32 triangles. Cut 4 – 4½" strips; subcut 64 – 2½" x 4½" rectangles. Cut 8 – 2½" strips; subcut 96 – 2½" x 2½" squares. Cut 3 – 2½" strips; use Side B to cut 64 HSTs.
Fabric #1—Red (includes binding)	1 yard	Cut 4 – 2½" strips; subcut 2 of the strips into 32 – 2½" x 2½" squares for the Chain blocks. Set aside the remaining 2 strips for the four-patch strip-sets. Cut 2 – 2½" strips; subcut 32 – 2½" x 2½" squares for Star blocks. Cut 8 – 2¼" strips for the binding.
Fabric #2—Aqua	⅓ yard	Cut 4 – 2½" strips; subcut 2 of the strips into 32 – 2½" x 2½" squares for the Chain blocks. Set aside the remaining 2 strips for the four-patch strip-sets.
Pink	1¼ yards	Cut 8 – 3½" strips; piece for the inner border. Cut 3 – 2½" strips; use Side B of EZ Flying Geese ruler to cut 64 HSTs.
Outer Border	2½ yards	Cut 4 – 5½" strips from LOF.
Backing	5¼ yards	Cut 2 panels 43" x 88".
Batting		88" x 88"

Get Set...

Relax and take your time to piece this quilt, which isn't a bit difficult to construct. There are three distinct blocks. You'll enjoy learning how to piece yet another, different style of Star block!

Sew!

Use 32 background fabric triangles and 32 triangles cut from the 9" squares to make large HST units. The units should measure 8½" x 8½". Square-up if necessary. Make the following combinations:

Make 8
Background/LIGHT

Make 16
Background/MEDIUM

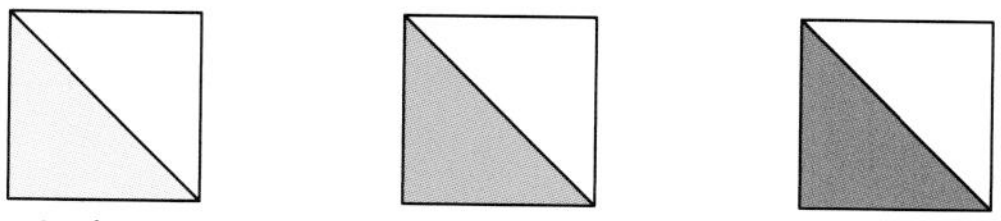

Make 8
Background/DARK

Make 2 strip-sets with the 2½" red and aqua fabric strips.

Rotate one strip-set and place RST on top of the other, butting the seams together and matching opposite fabrics. Cut into 16 – 2½" segments, keeping strip units RST.

Sew the segment pairs together along one edge; press each unit closed, then press the seam to one side. Make a total of 16 four-patch units.

The four-patch units should measure 4½" x 4½" unfinished. Square-up if necessary.

Make 16

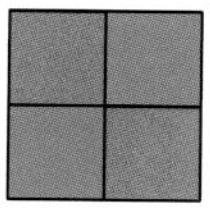

Sew 2 – 2½" x 4½" background fabric rectangles to opposite sides of all 16 four-patch units. Press the seams toward the rectangles.

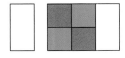

Make 16

Sew a red 2½" square and an aqua 2½" square to each end of a 2½" x 4½" background fabric rectangle. Press the seams toward the rectangles. Make 32 units.

Make 32

Add the rectangle units to four-patch units to complete the Chain blocks, paying close attention to the orientation of the corner fabric squares. Press the seams away from the four-patch units. Make 16.

The blocks should measure 8½" x 8½" unfinished. Square-up if necessary.

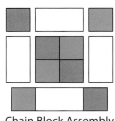

Chain Block Assembly
Make 16

For each Star block, use 4 Side B background fabric triangles and 4 Side B Jelly Roll fabric triangles to make 4 matching HST units (total 16 matching sets of 4 HST units each).

Press the seams toward Jelly Roll fabric triangles. The HST units should measure 2½" x 2½" unfinished. Square-up if necessary.

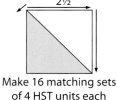

2½"

Make 16 matching sets of 4 HST units each

Draw a diagonal line on wrong side of 64 background 2½" x 2½" squares.

Place the marked background square RST on a 2½" x 4½" Jelly Roll rectangle.

Stitch on the drawn line, then trim ¼" from the stitching line.

Press the seam toward the background fabric triangle.

For each Star block, make 4 matching star point units (64 total).

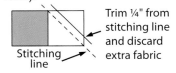

Trim ¼" from stitching line and discard extra fabric

Stitching line

Make 64 star point units

Make 16 different Star blocks, using matching sets of HST units and matching star point units of a different fabric within each block.

The Star blocks should measure 8½" x 8½" unfinished. Square-up if necessary.

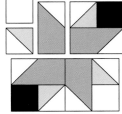

Make 16 Star blocks

Arrange the blocks into the layout as shown, being careful to rotate each block to achieve the desired layout. *(Remember my itty bitty mistake!)*

Use the darkest large HST units to form the inner diamond, the medium-large HST units to form the middle diamond, and lightest-large HST units to form the diagonal lines near the corners of quilt.

Sew the blocks into rows and joint the rows.

Add the borders.

Baste, quilt, bind, add a label, and enjoy!

Quilt Assembly

Thoughts About the Quilting

The large HST units were quilted with a combination of curves and tight roping. In the Star blocks, oval spirals that begin in the center and extend to the star tips were quilted, with a curved line traveling to the small triangles and extending to the respective tips. The quilting line curves and returns to the star's center in the same manner. Quilting spirals in the squares forming the "chain" was a great way to travel between the blocks and sections.

The background areas were symmetrical and identical, although some were cropped (in the corners) or mirrored. These background sections were the perfect place to add freehand feather quilting. To travel between the sections, stitch-in-the-ditch quilting was added around the stars and other geometric elements within the blocks.

For the border, the nested circles theme from the fabric itself was used as inspiration and circle guides were used to create the quilting design. The only real consideration was to distribute the circles evenly across the width of each border.

Try This: My favorite power snack pick-me-up

An enjoyable day of quilting actually requires quite a bit of stamina and you may find yourself running low on energy by late morning or mid-afternoon. Try my favorite go-to energy snack for a quick pick-me-up to sustain you while you finish your project! Simply combine fresh berries and cut up fresh fruit (whatever happens to be in season) and ½ cup of low-fat vanilla yogurt.

Okay, I confess: I'm a bit of a chocoholic. Although most of the time I do try to choose healthy snack foods, sometimes I just have to indulge my sweet tooth with my favorite chocolate treat: Wilbur Buds.

LOVELY LITTLE LEFTOVERS

Half-Square Triangle Design Dynamos—make the most of all those leftover bits!

Years ago, long before I began to teach quilting classes, I began a tradition. With every new quilt or project I challenged myself to learn at least one new technique, try one new thing, or develop one new skill. After all, even the experts need to continue to grow and improve their minds and skills by stretching their creative muscles! I've continued this exercise to this day!

As part of my challenge, I learn a difficult technique or perhaps I simply test a new product, use a different accessory foot for my sewing machine, or try a new specialty thread on my project and use it effectively. But at the very least I do at least one thing that is new for me.

When I began working with Jelly Roll strips I found there were almost always leftover bits that began to fill my scrap basket. So I devised a clever little project to go

hand in hand with my personal challenge: To use those leftover strips and bits to make what I like to call "Lovely Little Leftovers" from half-square triangles.

This has turned into such a fun and exciting exercise that I truly look forward to doing it whenever I finish a project!

The guidelines are simple:

◎ Use 80 – 2½" HST units, plus 40 – 2½" squares.

◎ Use the same layout each time, 8 x 10, with a pieced border of 2½" squares.

◎ Use the HST units to create a new layout or use a different machine-quilting technique.

That's it! And I've had such a ball making these little Jelly Roll quilted Bitlets! They are easy, fast, and a fantastic way for me to improve my skills. I hope you'll try them, too!

Quilted Bitlets Gallery
20" x 24", made by the author

Sew!

I'd like to encourage you to challenge yourself. Here are a few ideas to get you started:

 Try a variety of different design layouts with the 80 HST units.

◎ Use different decorative stitches on your machine you've never tried before to quilt your Bitlet.

◎ Use the maxi stitches on your machine to add motif quilting.

◎ Try a variety of new threads such as holographic, heavy 12-wt. cotton, variegated, neon, or glow-in-the-dark threads.

◎ Practice your free-motion machine quilting. Try freehand feathers, sign your name, etc.

◎ Bind your Bitlet by machine—sew the binding on the back side and stitch it in place on the front using a decorative or buttonhole stitch.

◎ Make small projects and gifts such as placemats, tote bags, table runners, hot pads, or ornaments.

◎ Trade the leftover strips with your friends or organize a Jelly Roll strip swap with your guild members.

◎ Save all the leftover strips until you have enough to make a large, ultra-scrappy quilt for your bed.

◎ Make charity quilts or rag rugs.

◎ Stuff pillows with the really little bits I like to call "schniblets."

Quilted Bitlet Layout

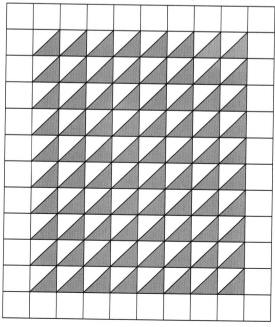

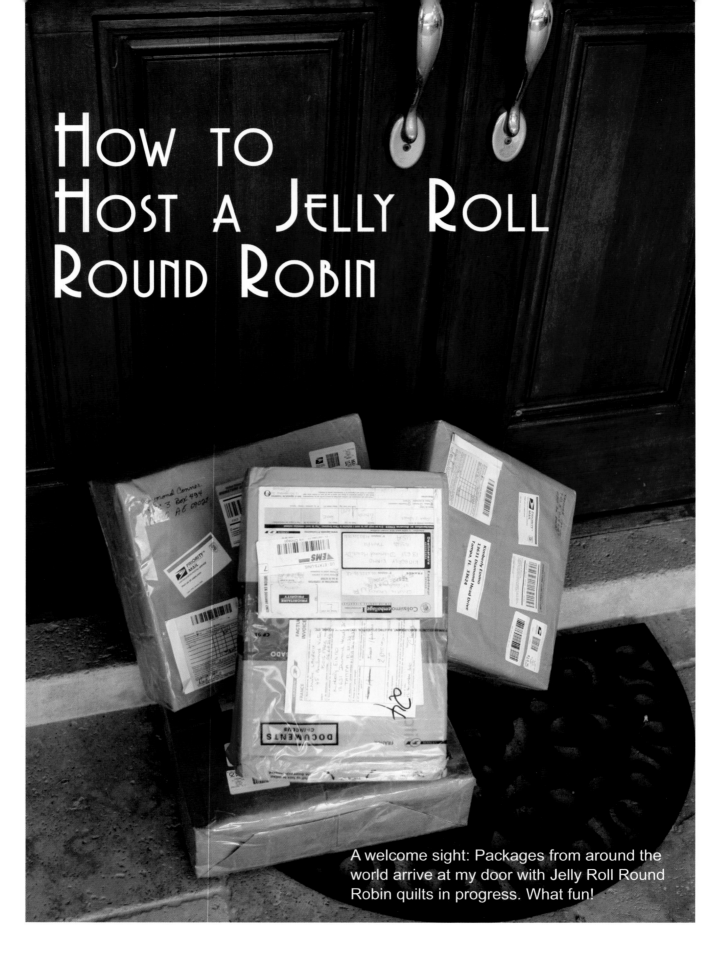

How to Host a Jelly Roll Round Robin

A welcome sight: Packages from around the world arrive at my door with Jelly Roll Round Robin quilts in progress. What fun!

In my previous book, *Jelly Roll Quilts and More*, I included instructions on hosting a Jelly Roll retreat. I was thrilled at the level of excitement and number of positive responses and emails I received from quilters everywhere telling me they were hosting their own Jelly Roll Retreats! So, as I began designing the quilts for this book, I wanted to continue the tradition of featuring a Fun With Friends Event.

I thought it would be wonderful to collaborate with my dear quilting friends from around the world by hosting our very own Jelly Roll Round Robin quilt challenge! This was easy to do and so much fun. And you can do it, too! All you need are a few willing pals (locally, nationally, or for all you quilters out there who blog—why not issue an international challenge?)

Exactly what is a Round Robin?

Typically, a round robin begins with every participant making a center block. The block gets passed to the next person in line who adds a border. The quilt is passed forward to the next participant who adds another border, and so on. A Jelly Roll Round Robin challenge would also work well with a row quilt format where the starting

point is a row of blocks and each participant adds a row instead of a border. (We had so much fun we're doing a Row by Row challenge next.) The choice is up to you!

The Challenge

Create quilts using 1 Jelly Roll, 1 matching Charm Pack, plus 1 background fabric per person.

The Guidelines

We chose Fandango by Lila Tueller, Moda Fabrics, as our Jelly Roll fabric line.

Each participant began by creating a 20½" x 20½" (unfinished) block in any style, using any method. The block was sent to the next person for a border to be added using any of the remaining fabrics in that participant's package.

Each person created a border, in turn, for each quilt and agreed to a schedule of approximately two weeks to work on each quilt.

No additional fabrics could be added (except binding). Borders were made using the fabrics from the original Jelly Roll and Charm Square pack.

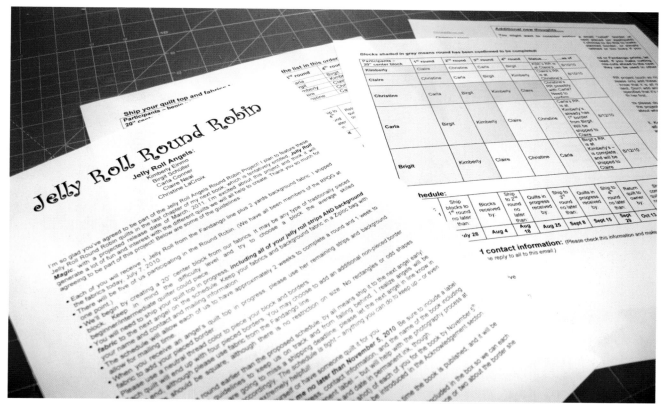

The Schedule

As an example, this was our shipping schedule.

Participants began with the center block	1st round	2nd round	3rd round	4th round
Kimberly	Claire	Christine	Carla	Birgit
Claire	Christine	Carla	Birgit	Kimberly
Christine	Carla	Birgit	Kimberly	Claire
Carla	Birgit	Kimberly	Claire	Christine
Brigit	Kimberly	Claire	Christine	Carla

Fabric received by each participant by:	Ship blocks to 1st round no later than:	Blocks received by:	Ship to 2nd round no later than:	Quilts in progress received by:	Ship to 3rd round no later than:	Quilts in progress received by:	Ship to 4th round no later than:	Return quilt top to owner by:
July 14	July 28	Aug 4	Aug 18	Aug 25	Sept 8	Sept 15	Sept 29	Oct 13

You can see that we allowed for shipping time since the participants were scattered around the globe. They were:

Claire Neal
Great Britain

Christine LaCroix,
France

Birgit Schüller
Germany

Carla Conner
The Netherlands

Yours truly
USA

I met each of these amazing, talented women through the Rheinland Pfalz Quilt Guild at Ramstein Air Base in Ramstein, Germany. I thought it would be fun to unite these women representing five different nationalities for this Jelly Roll Round Robin—to share our love for quilting and Jelly Rolls, and to span the miles between us, because we have since moved to different countries. We have kept in frequent contact while sharing photos, ideas, and progress reports through emails, phone calls, and regular Internet Skype sessions.

The Results

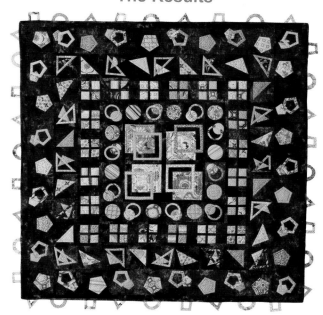

BIRGIT'S QUILT, 70" x 70"

Birgit suggested she use a brown fabric for her quilt to show how the same fabric line would look completely different with a dark background. She began with a modern, geometric design for her center square—a theme we all challenged ourselves to continue using while adding appliquéd geometric shapes.

CHRISTINE'S QUILT, 44" x 44"

Christine used folded fabrics in her center block so we each chose to continue her theme by adding three-dimensional elements including fabric origami, Prairie Points, and even beaded embellishments. This created a stunning quilt with lots of texture and interest.

CARLA'S QUILT, 80" x 80"

A Tree of Life block surrounded by leaves and trees, Flying Geese, stars, and a twinkling border complete this pretty nature theme.

CLAIRE'S QUILT, 64" x 64"

Claire began with a 20" Star block with diagonal lines, but interestingly, as we each added our borders, we couldn't tell where one border stopped and the next one began. This quilt looks like a single planned design. Delightful!

KIMBERLY'S QUILT, 57" x 57"

I used diamonds cut from Jelly Roll strips to make a variation of a Split Lemoyne Star design for my center block. I love the way each participant used unique and clever border treatments that complement and balance the overall design with an effective use of color. Each border is as unique and special as their friendship is to me!

An Invitation to Fun!

Invite as many friends as you'd like, but keep in mind someone will need to organize the effort and act as the facilitator. This isn't hard to do but you will need to keep track of the location and the status of each quilt in progress. (See the chart we used, page 86.)

I think an ideal group size is between five and six. If more than six participants are involved you may need to limit the width of each border added or consider creating individual blocks or a row-by-row quilt. For our Round Robin with only five participants, we were all shocked at just how large our quilts became by the end of the challenge.

Decisions, Decisions

You can either announce the fabric line you wish to use, vote for the majority's favorite, or have participants use 40 of their own fabrics to create their own precut bundle. Once my four friends accepted, I sent links to various websites with a choice of 5 different Jelly Rolls so they could vote for their favorite bundle. What's important is

that each fabric bundle stays with the same quilt so the fabrics used in each border will end up being balanced in the overall quilt.

We voted and I got a bolt of background fabric and sent each participant 2 yards. We soon discovered we all needed more than we had anticipated. Four yards of background fabric is a much better estimate of how much it will take to get the quilt finished with plenty of room for a fudge factor (goofs do happen).

Decide if there are technique or size restrictions. You've heard it before—KISS: "Keep It Simple, Sweetie." Guidelines and rules are fine, but don't make your list look like a legal document. This is supposed to be F-U-N for everyone. Define the general guidelines and then keep the door open for flexibility and fresh ideas.

Here are some great suggestions from what we learned from experience as you plan your own Jelly Roll Round Robin:

- Set deadlines. You'll need a start and end date, along with a reasonable amount of time for each participant to work on each quilt. I recommend 2–3 weeks with at least 1 week between to allow for shipping. If you make the deadlines too far apart, people will become distracted and lose interest (or worse, lose track of the project!)

- Decide up front whether these projects are meant to be a surprise for the recipients or if you plan to share progress reports and updates. For our Round Robin, half the fun was seeing and discussing the quilts in progress. We sent photos of quilts through email. This also allowed for an interesting exchange of dialogue when we hit a sticking point over our design ideas.

- Compile a sheet with all the participants' contact information including mailing addresses, phone numbers, email addresses, and so on. Keep it updated throughout the process in case there are any changes.

- Have everyone put their quilt-in-progress and all of the fabrics in large plastic storage bags and include a spool of piecing thread. This keeps everything protected and all in one place—easy to store, easy to ship.

While we had originally planned to use only 2½" strips, we soon discovered it would really expand our options if we could supplement our Jelly Rolls with a matching Charm Square pack.

Send out periodic updates. I kept a chart up-to-date at all times so I could keep track of the status and location of each and every Round Robin quilt.

Don't forget a label! Include a piece of stabilized fabric for each person to sign in your parcel. For fun, Birgit had everyone "ink" one of their fingers and include a "fingerprint" on her label along with each participant's signature. For my quilt label, I asked everyone to include a postage stamp from their respective country. When I received all the stamps, I scanned and printed them to fabric and included a handwritten message from each of them on my label. What a treasure for years to come!

Make notes and take digital photos. Although we were very lucky that all our quilts eventually arrived going back and forth across the Atlantic Ocean, there were a few tense days when a package or two seemed to be lost in the mail. Yikes! Make sure you follow customs procedures if you ship internationally and keep track of your shipping receipts. Insure the packages against loss or damage and pay extra to track the packages if possible. It's a good idea to say a little prayer when you ship, too.

Wise Words

Just Do It. Don't just think about it—make plans and get going. For me and my international friends, this was a special bonding experience that transcended borders (both of quilts and countries) and strengthened friendships forged over time and the many miles between us.

In our own words…

Birgit Schüller: "This Round Robin challenge was truly a global undertaking. It was exciting to find out what others are inspired by when creating their borders and which aspects caused me to decide what style border to add to their respective projects. I love to collaborate with friends

internationally, although this means dealing with various postal carriers and customs regulations and can be nerve-wrecking at times! But in the end, it was worth it!"

Carla Conner: "For me, the most challenging part was to create a border different from the other quilts but still matching the style of the quilt you were working on! The surprising part was seeing all the different patterns and blocks you could make from Jelly Roll strips and 5" squares! But the most fun was to watch the RR's grow into gorgeous quilts!"

Christine LaCroix: "I thought it was challenging to work on a quilt for someone I didn't know very well in person, but in the end seeing that the quilts came out beautifully. I was most surprised by all the three-dimensional elements on my quilt because I didn't really think about it when I made my original block. The best part of all was seeing that quilters in different countries are really all the same—crazy!"

Claire Neal: "Working on these Round Robin quilts was certainly a challenge! My only other experience with a group project was a row-by-row that I absolutely hated when I got it back; so I was a little hesitant about how this would turn out. I was also challenged by the fabrics we chose and the math involved. There were some very funky measurements in this challenge! However, I was happy to be asked to be part of it. As for my quilt, it doesn't look like a Round Robin project at all, but instead a well-planned design. It grew from my original block into a wonderful design. Given our geographical locations, mail restrictions, and summer vacations, kids, grandkids, etc., it's amazing what we achieved!"

Kimberly: As for me, I feel grateful and incredibly blessed that these talented women, who all have busy lives and careers of their own, took time to participate and play along while we forged ahead with a new idea. It was an amazing journey and so inspiring to see how they raised the bar with each round of the process. They challenged me far beyond what I expected the end results to be! Each of the quilts is so incredibly beautiful and so "fitting" to each one's personality. I'm simply thrilled with how they all turned out!

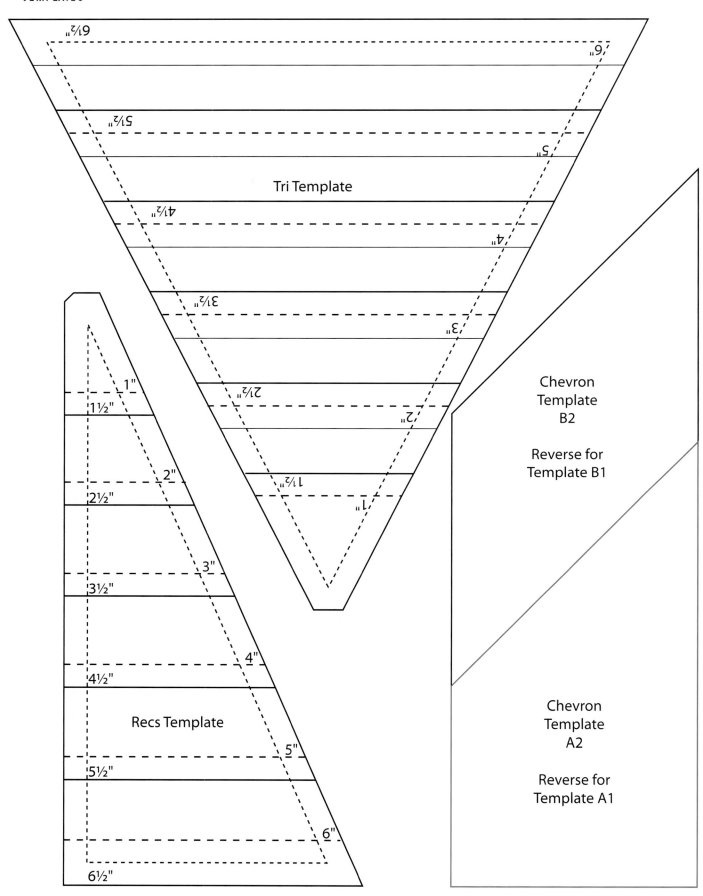

Tri Template

6½"
6"
5½"
5"
4½"
4"
3½"
3"
2½"
2"
1½"
1"

Recs Template

1"
1½"
2"
2½"
3"
3½"
4"
4½"
5"
5½"
6"
6½"

Chevron
Template
B2

Reverse for
Template B1

Chevron
Template
A2

Reverse for
Template A1

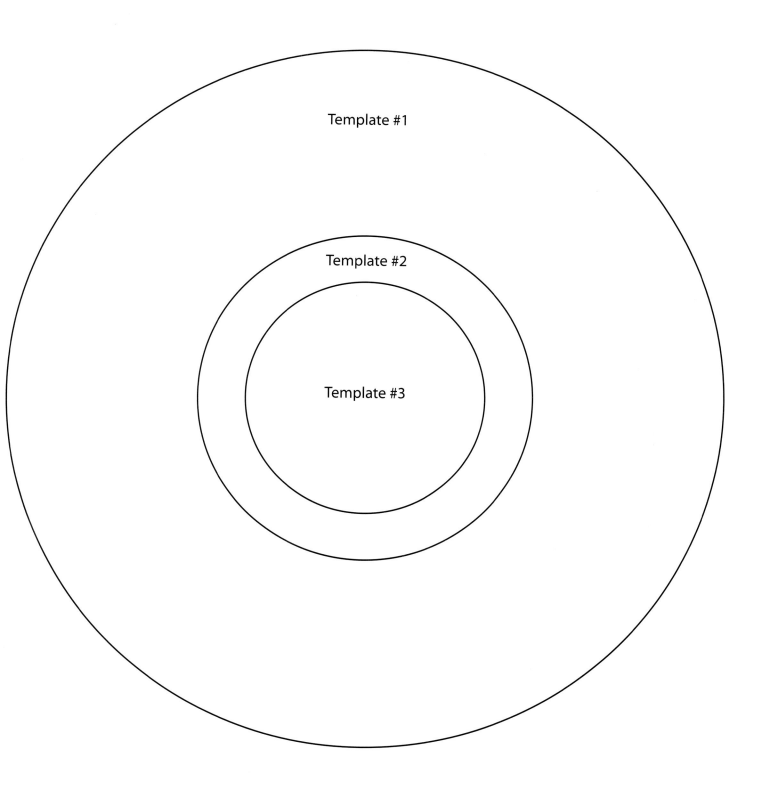

Template #1

Template #2

Template #3

JELLY ROLL MAGIC QUILTS SHOPPING LIST

Quilt	Size	Requirements	Additional Fabric	Fabric Line	Ruler Recommended
LONE STARBURST	65" x 65"	1 Jelly Roll	Background, binding	Cherish Nature by Deb Strain, Moda	EZ Jelly Roll Ruler
CHECKERBORDER RAINBOW STAR	24" x 24"	1 Jelly Roll	Background, binding	Fabric Freedom Noodles	EZ Jelly Roll Ruler
RAINBOW GEESE CROSSING	56" x 56"	1 Jelly Roll	Background, one contrasting fabric, binding	Robert Kaufman batik bundle brights	EZ Flying Geese
SPINNING SPOOLS	64" x 82"	1 Jelly Roll or 1 Layer Cake	Background, one contrasting fabric, outer border, binding	Selections of rainbow fabrics assembled by local shop	EZ Flying Geese
SPRING FLING	48" x 48"	1 Jelly Roll or 1 Layer Cake	Background, binding	Hunky Dory by Chez Moi, Moda	EZ Flying Geese EZ Jelly Roll Ruler
DELECTABLE DELIGHTS	48" x 48"	1 Jelly Roll or 1 Layer Cake	Background, inner and outer border, binding	A Breath of Avignon, Moda	EZ Flying Geese EZ Jelly Roll Ruler
SUMMER SPARKLERS	54" x 70"	1 Jelly Roll 1 Layer Cake	Background, contrasting fabric, inner, outer border, binding	Nautical and Nice by Sandy Gervais, Moda	EZ Flying Geese EZ Jelly Roll Ruler
LEAVES IN THE PUMPKIN PATCH	54" x 54"	1 Jelly Roll or 1 Layer Cake	Background, contrasting fabric, binding	Gobble, Gobble by Sandy Gervais, Moda	EZ Flying Geese EZ Jelly Roll Ruler
STARRY PINES	64" x 64"	2 Jelly Rolls 1 Charm Pack or 1 Layer Cake	Background, two contrasting fabrics, binding	Candy Land, Moda	EZ Flying Geese EZ Jelly Roll Ruler
JUST DOTTY	58" x 72"	1 Jelly Roll 1 Layer Cake or 2 Layer Cakes	Background, fabric, binding	Origins by Basicgray, Moda	Template, page 91 or EZ Circle Cut Tool EZ Jelly Roll Ruler
FAUX CATHEDRAL WINDOWS, LARGE	70" x 70"	1 Layer Cake	Two contrasting fabrics, inner and outer borders, binding	Clermont Farms by Minick and Simpson, Moda	Template, page 70
FAUX CATHEDRAL WINDOWS, SMALL	34" x 34"	1 Charm Pack	Two contrasting fabrics for blocks, outer border, binding	Tranquility by Sandy Gervais, Moda	Template, page 70
STICKS & STONES	78" x 86"	2 Jelly Rolls or 1 Layer Cake & 1 Jelly Roll	Contrasting fabric, binding	Lollipop by Sandy Gervais, Moda	EZ Jelly Roll Ruler
SHOOTING STARS	80" x 80"	1 Jelly Roll 1 Layer Cake	Background, contrasting fabric, border, binding	Bliss by Bonnie and Camille, Moda	EZ Flying Geese EZ Jelly Roll Ruler

Resources

Contributors

It is with sincere appreciation and a grateful heart I wish to thank the following companies for their support of products and services which helped to make this book possible. The fabric, batting, tools and supplies featured or mentioned in this book are some of my personal favorites and can be purchased at your local quilt shop, sewing machine dealer, on the Internet or by mail order.

Moda Fabrics / United Notions
For generously providing much of the fabric used to make the quilts in this book
13800 Hutton Drive
Dallas, TX 75234
Phone: 800-527-9447
Web: www.unitednotions.com

Robert Kaufman Fabrics
For generously providing fabric
129 West 132nd Street
Los Angeles, CA 90061
Phone: 800-877-2066
Web: www.robertkaufman.com

Fairfield Processing Corp.
For generously providing all the batting used to make the quilts featured in this book
P.O. Box 1157
Danbury, CT 06813-1157
Phone: 800-980-8000
Web: www.poly-fil.com

YLI Threads
For generously providing many of the threads used to make the quilts featured in this book
1439 Dave Lyle Blvd.
Rock Hill, SC 29730
Phone: 803-985-3100
Web: www.ylicorp.com

BERNINA of America
Sewing machines and accessories
3702 Prairie Lake Court
Aurora, IL 60504
Phone: 630-978-2500
Web: www.berninausa.com

American Quilter's Society
My favorite publisher of this and other top quality quilting books
P.O. Box 3290
Paducah, KY 42002-3290
Phone: 270-898-7903
Web: www.americanquilter.com

Electric Quilt Company
EQ7 and other quilting software products
419 Gould Street, Suite 2
Bowling Green, OH 43402-3047
Phone: 419-352-1134
Web: www.electricquilt.com

Rowenta USA
Irons and steamers
2199 Eden Road
Millville, NJ 08332
Phone: 800-ROWENTA
Web: www.rowentausa.com

The Simplicity Creative Group
Quilting rulers, tools, and notions
6050 Dana Way
Antioch TN 37013
Phone: 800-545-5740
Web: www.ezquilt.com

Prym Consumer USA, Inc.
Omnigrid rulers and cutting mats
P.O. Box 5028
Spartanburg, SC 29304
Web: www.dritz.com/brands/omnigrid/index.php

Olfa-North America
Rotary cutters, blades and mats
5500 N. Pearl St.
Rosemont, IL 60018
Phone: 800-962-OLFA
Web: www.olfa.com

Sulky of America
Threads, stabilizers
960 Cobb Place Blvd.
Kennesaw, GA 30144
Phone: 800-874-4115
Web: www.sulky.com

Clover Needlecraft Inc.
*Sewing, quilting notions, and tools
including Yo-Yo Makers!*
1441 S. Carlos Ave.
Ontario, CA 91761
Phone: 800-233-1703
Web: www.clover-usa.com

Kim Brunner
Machine quilting guides and more
web: http://kimmyquilt.com

Schmetz
Sewing machine needles
3800 W. 42nd St.
Chicago, IL 60632
Web: www.schmetz.com

Jilily Studio Needle Arts
Appliqué glue
11626 Sunset Hills Dr.
Highland, UT 84003
Phone: 801-234-9884
Web: www.jililystudio.com

ArtBin Storage Products
ArtBin plastic satchels
Web: www.artbin.com
Phone: 800-232-3474

Longarm Machine Quilting Services
Birgit Schüller
Creative BiTS
Schachtstrasse 5
66292 Riegelsberg
Germany
Phone: +49 (6806) 920 447
Email: birgit.schueller@creativebits.biz
Web: www.creativebits.biz

Carolyn Archer
Ohio Star Quilting
2895 Wilmington Road
Lebanon, OH 45036
Phone: 513-933-9008
Email: carcher3@roadrunner.com

Christine LaCroix
Quilt Patch Deco Quilting
9 Alleé des Tournesols
64600 Anglet
France
Phone: 33(0)9 81 28 74 20
Email: Christine@quiltpatchdeco.com
Web: www.quiltpatchdeco.com

Photography
Alisha Pergola Photography
Web: http://www.alishapergolaphotography.com
Email: Alisha@alishapergolaphotography.com

About the Author

Photo by Alisha Pergola Photography

Kimberly Einmo is an author, designer, judge, and international quilting instructor. Her first two books, *Quilt A Travel Souvenir* and the best-selling *Jelly Roll Quilts & More*, were published by the American Quilter's Society. Kimberly's original quilt designs and numerous articles have appeared in a wide variety of publications including *McCall's Quilting* and *McCall's Quick Quilts* magazines, *American Quilter* magazine, *Japanese Patchwork Tsushin* magazine, *Irish Quilting* magazine, *Quilter's Home* and *Quilt Life* magazine. She has developed several innovative and exciting acrylic tools including the EZ Jelly Roll Ruler, EZ Flying Geese ruler, EZ Hearts Cut Tool, and EZ Pineapple Ruler. Her popular and highly successful series of Mystery Quilts are in high demand by students everywhere.

Kimberly has judged many prestigious quilt contests and has taught at many more international, national, and regional quilt conferences and shows. To date, she has been the only instructor invited to represent the United States at the Annual Prague Patchwork Meeting where she was the guest instructor in 2008 and 2010.

Asked back by popular demand, she'll return to the Czech Republic to teach at the PPM in 2012. Kimberly has taught classes on many quilting cruises including destinations to the Caribbean, Mexico, and Alaska. She has appeared as a repeat guest on the PBS series *America Quilts Creatively*.

Kimberly is part of the elite group of American Sewing Professionals who represent the BERNINA Company throughout the US and abroad and she has also represented Pfaff as one of the VSM Sewing Stars since 2005. She loves to share her passion and enthusiasm for quilting with people everywhere.

Kimberly has been married to her best friend for more than twenty-three years to Kent, a retired U.S. Air Force officer who now works as a government contractor in the field of Information Technology. They have two handsome sons, Joshua and Andrew. As a family, they love to travel in the US and abroad and take every opportunity to get out and see the world! To complete their happy family, they have one very pampered pooch, Divot, and three exceptional cats, Tuffy, Poppy, and Snickers, who can be found keeping Kimberly company (adding fiber content to her quilts—80% cotton, 20% cat hair) in the studio while she creates.

You can order Kimberly's specialty tools directly from her at her website: **www.kimberlyeinmo.com.**

EZ Flying Geese ruler (formerly known as the Easy Star & Geese Ruler). This new design enables you to cut 10 sizes instead of 9. Either ruler can be be used as described in the text.

EZ Jelly Roll Ruler (formerly known as the Simpli-EZ Jelly Roll Ruler)

EZ Hearts Cut Tool

EZ Pineapple Ruler

MORE AQS BOOKS

This is only a small selection of the books available from the American Quilter's Society. AQS books are known worldwide for timely topics, clear writing, beautiful color photos, and accurate illustrations and patterns. The following books are available from your local bookseller, quilt shop, or public library.

#8146

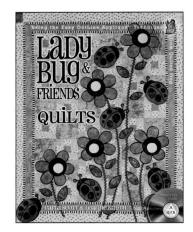

#8351

#8528

#8349

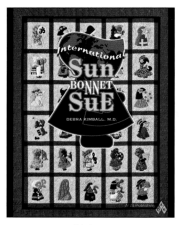

#8347

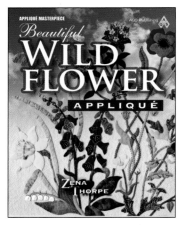

#8526

#8355

#8355

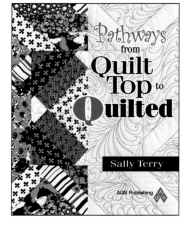

#8348

LOOK for these books nationally.
CALL or VISIT our website at

1-800-626-5420
www.AmericanQuilter.com